PLANNING TO REMEMBER

Also by Fiona McPherson

My Memory Journal

Perfect Memory Training

Easy Russian Alphabet: A Visual Workbook

Indo-European Cognate Dictionary

Mnemonics for Study (2nd ed.)

Successful Learning Simplified: A Visual Guide

How to Approach Learning: What teachers and students should know about succeeding in school

How to Learn: The 10 principles of effective practice and revision

Effective Notetaking (3rd ed.)

The Memory Key

Planning to Remember

How to remember what you're doing and what you plan to do

Fiona McPherson, PhD

Wayz Press
Wellington, New Zealand

Published 2010 by Wayz Press, Wellington, New Zealand.

Copyright © 2010 by Fiona McPherson.

All rights reserved.

No part of this publication may be reproduced, stored in a retrieval system, or transmitted in any form or by any means, electronic, mechanical, recording or otherwise, without the prior written permission of Wayz Press, a subsidiary of Capital Research Limited.

ISBN 978-0-9876522-6-3

To report errors, please email errata@wayz.co.nz

For additional resources and up-to-date information about any errors, go to the Mempowered website at www.mempowered.com

Contents

Why read this book?   1

1. **How memory works and why it sometimes fails**   5
   - Memories are made of this   5
   - Why people fail to remember   8
   - Know thyself: a quiz   11

2. **Remembering to do things**   17
   - Memory for future actions is different from other types of memory   17
   - Retrospective memory   22
   - Forgetting routine actions is not a failure of memory   22

3. **Short-term goals and short-term memory**   25
   - Working memory   25
   - Working memory and attention   28
   - Age and attention   33

4. **Forgetting what you're doing**   37
   - Short-term memory problems are attention problems   38
   - Action sequences are why we make action slips   40

Common types of action slip	45
Situations when action slips are most likely	48
Have I done it already?	52
What makes some people more prone to absent-minded errors?	54
How to prevent action slips	56

5. Structuring your goals 63

A hierarchy of goals	63
Ordering your goals	66
The problem of suspended intentions	67

6. Circumstances that affect your remembering 71

Event-based retrieval cues are better than time-based	72
Is being too busy a valid excuse?	75
Wanting to remember is not enough!	76
Timing and complexity	77

7. Are some people better at remembering intentions? 84

Age differences	84
Individual differences	87
Review	94

8. General strategies for remembering intentions 95

Strategies people use — 95
Effective strategies for remembering intentions — 97
Mental strategies for better recall — 97
Using environmental memory aids — 109

9. Strategies for specific tasks — 112
Remembering appointments — 113
Remembering anniversaries and birthdays — 118
Remembering arrangements — 123
Remembering errands and chores — 126
Remembering to take medicine — 129
Summary of memory tasks & appropriate strategies — 135

10. Your master strategy — 137
Assessing memory tasks — 137
Deciding on your memory strategies — 141

11. It's not all about memory — 145
We fail to achieve intentions for many reasons — 145
Believing in your abilities — 153
The bottom line — 155

Appendix A: Theories of prospective memory — 157
Appendix B: External memory aids — 165
Appendix C: The coding mnemonic — 169

Appendix D: Specific strategies for specific tasks	171
Glossary of terms	173
Chapter Notes	177
References	184

Why read this book?

What this book is about

Have you ever forgotten someone's birthday? An appointment? To pick up the milk on the way home? To take your medication? To turn the stove off? Why you've come into a room?

Of course you have. This sort of forgetting is common to all of us — though some are more prone to it than others.

Research suggests that failures of prospective memory (which is what this kind of memory is called) account for at least half, and perhaps as many as 80%, of all everyday memory failures.

So should we worry about them?

Well, it depends. Prospective memory failures can be embarrassing, hurtful, and sometimes dangerous. Even at their best, they're an annoyance. But because of the nature of this type of memory, a certain level of failure must be accepted. What's important is where those failures occur. The purpose of this book is to help you reduce the number of failures and restrict them to those areas that are less important to you. I also hope it will help you become more relaxed about the failures you do have!

What this book should do for you

The world is full of self-help books, and despite the grandiloquent claims they tend to make, few of them change many people's lives permanently. To truly benefit from such a book, you need to have very specific and focused aims, or all you'll come away with is a feeling that you have learned something (what we might call the 'feel-good' factor). But if you can't clearly put into words what you've learned and precisely how you're going to apply it, your chances of lasting benefit are small.

So what should you aim to get out of this book?

Studies have shown that even month-long, intensive memory improvement courses rarely result in long-lasting memory improvement — because improving your memory isn't simply a matter of learning some memory strategies. You also need to understand how and when to apply them. Those who are most likely to benefit from instruction in specific techniques are those who understand how memory works.

So your first goal should be to understand how this particular kind of memory works. Specifically:

How prospective memory is different from other types of memory.

Why prospective memory is more prone to failure than other types of memory.

When prospective memory failures are most likely.

The second goal, of course, is to learn effective memory strategies for dealing with, or preventing, these types of failures. In this book, you'll:

- Learn how specific tasks are different from each other.
- Choose which specific tasks you wish to do better at.
- Find out which strategies are effective for those particular tasks, and which of these are most suited to you.

The third goal is the least obvious. You need to acquire faith. Do you know what the most important factor is in determining how good your memory is? It's not how smart you are. It's not whether you've got good "memory genes". It's whether or not you use effective memory strategies. And whether you do *that* depends on whether you:

- see a need (recognize your own failings), *and*
- have faith that memory strategies actually work.

Recognizing the need is harder than you might think. Why doesn't a student work harder to learn new information? Because they think they have worked hard enough! Why don't people make more of an effort to remember a new name, a joke, a story they've just been told? Because they believe the memory is strong enough without that effort.

A lot of the time, they're wrong.

Then there's the question of belief. You've perhaps come across the problem in some other situation. Maybe in trying to lose weight, or managing your inbox, or raising the performance of your team. Whatever it is, did you have a little voice in your head that said, "Well, this isn't going to work." And chances are it won't!

Even if it does seem to work initially, if you weren't totally convinced in the value of your strategy, chances are you didn't keep it up. Believing in what you're doing is vital.

So part of my goal is to convince you that these strategies do work.

Let's start with a quick run-through of the basics of how memory works (I explain them in more detail in my books *The Memory Key* and *Perfect Memory Training*).

How memory works and why it sometimes fails

Memories are made of this

Memories are codes

Memory is commonly portrayed as if it is a photographic record, as if everything we have ever experienced is faithfully recorded, blow by separate, exquisitely detailed, blow. But this isn't true, and if you are to improve your memory skills you need to understand that this is not true. You need to understand that memory is not complete, and is not a replication.

Memory is selected.

Selected, twisted, constructed, and re-constructed.

And very personal.

I like to talk of "memory codes" rather than "memories", because it constantly reminds us that memories have been created — that *we* have created them.

> Memory is a network of codes. We create the codes, and whether or not we can find them again (remember them) depends on how well we constructed them.

My memory code for "cat" is different from your memory code for "cat", although both of us agree on what a cat is. Mine will include information about Pushti, a black part-Persian, with a lovely fluffy tail, that was the first family cat I remember. It includes memories of Dinah Pyewacket, my grandparents' cat — a Siamese who had farex (a sort of baby porridge) for breakfast, and used to sit on my grandfather's knee in the evening. It includes my opinions of cats (kittens are of course adorable, but I'm more of a dog person), my (limited and probably inaccurate) knowledge of Egyptian cat-goddesses, the kinesthetic memory of a cat's claws, as well as "general knowledge" about cats — that they're mammals, that they're furry, that they come in numerous varieties, etc.

You and I will share much of that general knowledge, but it will all be colored by those individual, personal experiences of particular cats. If you have a cat of your own, then your memory code for "cat" will probably be dominated by those personal experiences. My personal experiences of cats are neither strong nor recent, and accordingly, in most circumstances, "cat" brings forth general rather than specific knowledge.

But circumstances are important. If I see a Siamese cat, I'm more likely to think of Dinah. If, as I did the other day, I see a cat sharpening her claws on a rug, I'm more likely to remember instead, Pushti, clawing our heavy living-room curtains to bits.

Memory codes — an example

To give you the flavor of a memory code, here is an example of part of a network of memory codes.

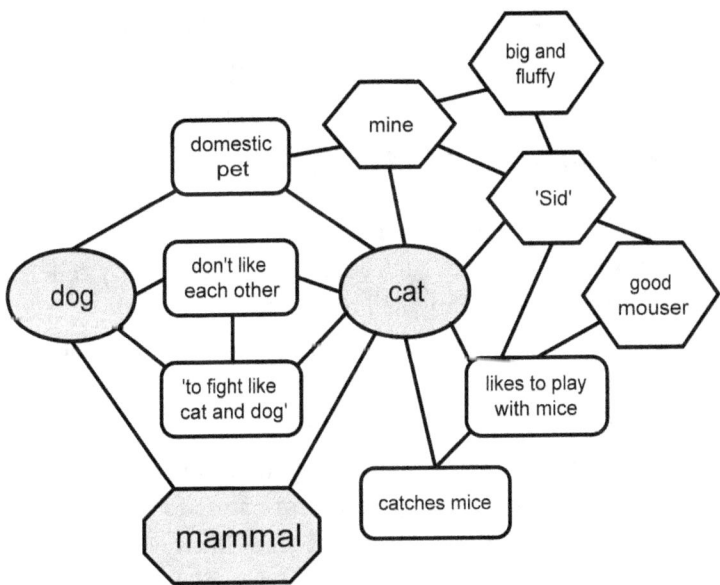

This is part of a possible memory code for 'cat'. Notice how 'dog', although a separate memory code, is included here, because of the strong association between cats and dogs. If you study the various bits of this network, you will realize how arbitrary the boundaries between codes are. My code for 'Sid' is presumably an entity in itself, and yet it merges inescapably with the more general code for 'cat', which itself is bound indissolubly with that of 'dog'. Parts of the code — like 'domestic pet' and 'mine' — are clearly part of other codes; that doesn't make them any less part of this one. Nor does it mean there's a huge amount of repetition in the system.

> Remembering depends on the links we make between codes — for we find a memory code by traveling the trails formed by the links.

What it does mean is that codes are collections of linked nodes, and strength of the links is all-important. And that strength will

How memory works

wax and wane over time, which means a memory code is not a static thing, but blown by the winds of context and experience.

What makes a code strong?

Links that are recent will be more easily remembered, and links are strengthened through repetition. So a memory code that you retrieve frequently will be much more easily remembered than one that you only retrieve occasionally (to the extent that you don't even think of it as remembering — the information is simply there when you need it).

Codes are also strengthened by being linked to other strong codes — which is why linking new information to information you already know well is such a good idea. To remember someone you've just met called Fred Bloggs will be helped if you link him in your mind to your cousin Fred or to your favorite blog.

How easily a memory code is found therefore depends on the strength of the memory code, which is affected not only by how often and how recently you have retrieved it, but also on the links you have made to other codes — which in turn depends on the particular information you have selected to encode (if you only encoded "Fred", you wouldn't be able to link to "blog").

> Improving your remembering is about building strong codes and strong links.

Why people fail to remember

Memory failures occur for a lot of reasons. But they don't occur simply because the memory task is difficult. Nor do they occur because the person is incapable of remembering —

although we are probably all guilty of berating ourselves or others as "hopeless at remembering (birthdays / names / jokes / …)".

But humans have a remarkable capacity for remembering and we all demonstrate that capacity repeatedly every day. Moreover, we all know at least *some* memory strategies that could help us remember.

The main problem isn't that we have a "poor memory", or that we don't know how to help ourselves remember. The main problem is that we *fail to realize we need help*.

Monitoring your memory

Monitoring your memory is an important — and often overlooked — memory strategy that underlies all memory skills. If you can't reliably gauge when information is properly stored in your memory, if you can't judge how well you have encoded it in memory and how easily it will be retrieved when required, then how will you recognize when you need to take further action to remember something?

> Recognizing when we need to use a memory strategy is the first and most important step in improving our memory.

Children in particular are extremely poor at monitoring their memory. While they are often confident of their ability to remember, this is not matched by their actual recall. Nor do they seem to recognize the need to take some action to help themselves remember. They remember it *now*, they reason, so why shouldn't they remember it later?

> To improve your memory, you must recognize when your memory needs help.

With time, they come to understand the fallibility of memory, and learn strategies for dealing with it. But of course, some people are better than others at developing an awareness of their needs and working out more effective skills. Even among college students, as many as a third may use no memory strategies in circumstances when they need to (not even a strategy as simple as repeating the information to themselves)[2].

Believing in your own abilities

There is another reason for failing to recognize the need for some sort of memory strategy — when you are convinced that your memory failures are because you have a "bad memory". This may be because you were repeatedly told this as a child and consequently your "bad memory" is simply, inescapably, part of who you are. Or it may be that this is something you feel has come upon you at some point in your life. Older adults in particular, are inclined to regard any memory failures as a result of their increasing age, and therefore inevitable.

But there is little relationship between the degree to which someone complains of her memory, and her memory performance. People who feel they have a general memory problem forget things no more frequently than people who *don't* see themselves as having a problem[3].

On the other hand, we are much more accurate when it comes to making judgments about our abilities at *specific* memory tasks[4]. Therefore, while statements such as "oh, I have a poor memory" should never be taken as gospel, statements such as "I'm just terrible at remembering names" are much more believable.

This doesn't mean, however, that you should ever make such statements about yourself! There is nothing carved in stone about your degree of skill at a task. And that is what we are talking about here — not *ability* (which sounds like something you are born with), but *skill* (which is something you acquire).

But before you can improve your skills, you need to know which skills need improving.

Know thyself: a quiz

So, what are *your* beliefs about your ability to remember what you're doing, what you intend to do, near and distant future events? Clearly you have some concerns, or you wouldn't be reading this book! But have you thought about the specifics of what you remember and what you don't?

The following questionnaire is designed to help you think about the specific memory tasks that involve intention memory, and to help you assess your memory performance. You may find it useful to add a priority rating to those memory tasks that are important to you.

1. In conversation, do you forget to bring up some point or question that you had intended to mention	never sometimes often
2. At the store, do you forget at least one of your intended items	never sometimes often
3. When going out to do some errands, do you forget to do at least one of them	never sometimes often
4. When taking medication, do you forget to take it at the right time	never sometimes often
5. Do you forget appointments	never sometimes often
6. Do you forget special dates (birthdays, anniversaries, etc)	never sometimes often
7. Do you forget promises you have made to other people	never sometimes often
7b. Think about the various people you might make promises to. How often do you forget promises made to:	
your spouse/partner	never sometimes often
your child(ren)	never sometimes often
other close relatives	never sometimes often
friends	never sometimes often
workmates	never sometimes often
your boss/client	never sometimes often

8. Do you forget to return borrowed items on time	never sometimes often
9. Do you forget routine chores (e.g., to water your plants, to take out the rubbish, to pay bills)	never sometimes often
10. Do you keep forgetting to do infrequent personal tasks (e.g., renewing a passport, making a doctor's appointment)	never sometimes often
11. Do you forget personal goals (e.g., setting aside time every day for a fitness/study activity, intentions to achieve some home maintenance or personal goal within a certain time)	never sometimes often
12. Do you forget work goals	never sometimes often
13. Do you have trouble remembering ideas that you've had	never sometimes often
14. If other people expect you to remember for them, do you forget other people's intentions	never sometimes often
15. Do you sometimes find yourself in a place and know that there is something you meant to do there, but you can't remember what it is	never sometimes often

16. Do you remember an intended action at an inappropriate time or place, and then forget it when the time/place is appropriate	never sometimes often
17. If so, does this happen within quite short time-spans (e.g., walking from one room to another)	never sometimes often
18. Do you forget to pass on messages/information to others	never sometimes often
19. Do you forget to terminate actions (taking things out of the oven; turning a hose off; picking up drycleaning, etc)	never sometimes often
20. Do you mix up familiar sequences of actions (e.g., putting milk & sugar in your cup but forgetting the coffee; putting sugar in twice; putting the coffee in your cereal bowl)	never sometimes often
21. Do you find yourself carrying out a familiar action you hadn't intended (e.g., going to your bedroom for a book, you start taking off your clothes)	never sometimes often
22. Do you carry out the right action on the wrong object (e.g., putting the butter in the dishwasher and the plate in the fridge)	never sometimes often

This isn't the kind of quiz you pass or fail, so I haven't provided a way to score. The object of this questionnaire is to get you thinking about your memory performance in this specific area — intention memory. You may look over your answers and think, "Oh dear, I'm worse than I thought!" Or you may think, "That's not so bad, I'm better than I thought I was!"

However, you can identify the areas in which you have particular problems by counting the number of times you marked "often" for each general task. Here you can see which questions relate to which types of memory problems:

A: short-term memory: 1, 15, 17, 19

B: retrospective memory: 2, 3, 13, 18 (for this last one, only count if it's the message itself you have trouble remembering, rather than the fact of having a message for the person)

C: time-based prospective memory: 4, 5, 6, 8

D: interpersonal issues: 6, 7, 14, 18

E: organizational & motivational issues: 10, 11, 12

F: event-based prospective memory: 16, 18

G: action slips: 9, 20, 21, 22

Don't worry if some, or indeed any, of these terms don't make much sense to you yet! They'll be explained during the course of this book. For now, just note if you have any particular problems in any of these areas, so that you'll be primed to pay special attention when I discuss them.

Part of the point of this exercise is to demonstrate how specific details often give quite a different picture from your global impression. The main point, however, is to get you thinking about the kinds of memory tasks there are, and in particular, the kinds of memory tasks that you specifically want to improve. With these in mind as you go through the book, you'll be better able to focus on what *you* need.

Later on, when we've looked at how intention memory works, and looked at effective strategies for remembering intentions, we'll come back to these tasks, and work out the most effective, very specific strategies, for dealing with these very specific tasks.

> ### Main points
>
> There is no such thing as a "bad memory".
>
> People who believe their memory is poor are generally no more forgetful than other people.
>
> To remember well, you need to have faith that you can.
>
> To remember well, you need to recognize when your memory needs assistance.
>
> To remember well, you need to learn how to build effective memory codes.

Remembering to do things

Memory for future actions is different from other types of memory

You may remember the names of all the latest Olympic gold medalists, but this doesn't make you reliable at remembering to pick up milk on the way home. Or at remembering your spouse's birthday. Or at remembering to make a dentist's appointment.

There is no relationship between your memory for facts, and your memory for future actions and intentions[5].

Memory is not a thing

Memory has been compared to a filing cabinet, a library, a computer. But memory is not simply a storage system. Memory is not a *thing*. Memory is a *process*.

Different types of information are treated in different ways. Does it make sense that the information *A Siamese is a type of cat* be processed and recorded in the same way as the memory of a piece of music? As the memory of the smell of Christmas lilies, that recalls to my mind my grandmother's house? As the knowledge that 1010 comes after 1009? As the knowledge that I planned to make quiche for tea?

We have memories that involve different senses. We have memories that involve the past and memories that involve the future. We have memories for facts, and memories of people, memories of our likes and desires and the things that have happened to us, memories of joy and grief and hunger and boredom.

Memories are of different types, and belong in different classes. These classes are termed **domains**. There is a domain for facts, a domain for people, a domain for events, a domain for skills, and a domain for future actions and events.

> Remembering intentions is different from other types of remembering.

To learn how to improve your memory for future plans, you need to understand how this particular type of memory is processed.

Remembering the past relies on triggers

Remembering information you have learned, or experiences you have had, people you have met, usually involves **retrieval cues** — things that trigger your remembering. The sight of a familiar face triggers your memory for the person whose face it is. The question "What's the capital of Australia?" triggers the stored information: "Canberra". Seeing your old school brings back memories of things that happened to you there.

Occasionally, a memory seems to pop into our heads for no apparent reason, but even then, there has been some triggering event — a barely noticed object, a casual thought.

Remembering your intentions is harder.

There are fewer triggers to help you remember the future

Remembering future actions and events cannot always wait upon cues to remind us. If we need to buy something, we can't always wait until we happen to be in an appropriate store and happen to see the desired object. We usually need to take action to get ourselves to the right store; we need to *look for* the object.

Remembering future intentions is triggered easily

Perhaps because of the paucity of retrieval cues, future memory tends to be more easily triggered than "normal" memory. The cues that remind us of future actions and events are often only marginally related to the task we're reminded of[6]. Seeing a container of flaxseed oil on the kitchen bench reminds me I meant to ring my partner (whose flaxseed oil it is) at his office. Seeing an envelope with a Suzuki logo on it reminds me I need to pay the bill for my son's piano lessons.

> Even distantly related things are often enough to remind us of future actions and events.

Why planning memory is more challenging than other memory tasks

Although the principal reason future memory can be problematic is the lack of reminder cues, there are other complicating factors as well. A major one is time — both the

Intentions must be remembered for an often lengthy period of time. length of time you need to remember for, and the specificity of time.

Remembering an intention over an hour, or a day, or a month, is not simply made harder by the passage of time, but also by the fact that during that time you will be engaged in other actions. You are not sitting waiting for the appropriate time to carry out your intention; you are busy with other tasks. These activities will of course use your memory as well. In some cases, they will even use that same memory domain. Thinking about these other activities, planning them, remembering them — all this will interfere with your remembering of this other intention.

And then there's the further complication: part of remembering a future action is not simply remembering the action, but also, remembering to do it *at a particular time*.

Consider this possible memory code for a dentist appointment:

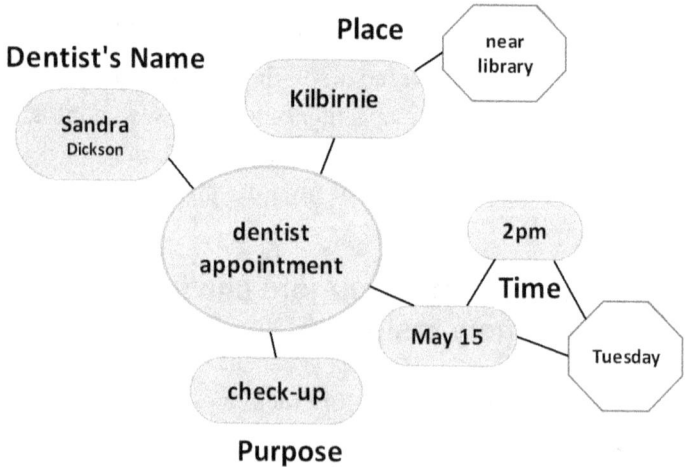

This is of course a grossly simplified representation, selecting the main points — in this case: place, time, other person involved, purpose.

What will trigger my remembering of this memory code? It could be the place — since the dentist is one of the few things I go to the suburb of Kilbirnie for, I never fail to be there without some awareness that my dentist is there. On the other hand, since I have few reasons to go there, what are the chances of being there to trigger this memory?

The name of the dentist might trigger remembering — if I ran across someone with the same first name or the same last name, for example. But again, what are the odds of that?

The core attribute of this memory code — dentist — is likely to be the strongest and most probable trigger. Seeing or hearing about anything to do with teeth or dentists is likely to trigger this memory code (i.e., remind me that I have a dentist appointment coming up). However, this is not necessarily all that useful.

For a memory code of this nature (an intended action), it is not enough to remember it. You must remember it at a particular time. It is the time part of the code then, that must be strong enough to trigger remembering.

You are often required to remember intentions at a specified time.

But time is the least informative cue there. Being in Kilbirnie will easily trigger my remembering; hearing or seeing the dentist's name will easily trigger my remembering. The time — which passes in a perfectly predictable and expected fashion — is not going to trigger anything unless I have put some effort into making it a cue.

Retrospective memory

The type of memory involved in remembering intentions is formally called prospective memory. But it does need to be remembered that successfully remembering to do something not only requires you to remember, at the right time, *that* you have to do something (prospective memory), it also requires you to remember *what* you have to do — which requires 'normal', **retrospective memory** (memory of the past).

This distinction is most clearly seen in the instance of having to remember to pass on a message to a friend. To do this successfully, you must remember not only to give her the message, but also the content of the message.

Interestingly, because there is little correlation between prospective and retrospective memory (you may be great at one and poor at the other), those who are good at remembering to pass on a message are not necessarily any better at remembering the message itself than those people who are poor at remembering to pass on messages[7].

> Remembering intended actions & events also involves normal "past" memory. It may be your retrospective memory that is the problem.

Forgetting routine actions is not a failure of memory

So, remembering, whether of the past (retrospective memory) or the future (prospective memory), relies on cues, which may be externally or internally generated. Cues, to be any good, must be noticed. That's why time is such a poor cue, because time passing is part of the background. To notice a specific time, we have to make an effort to distinguish it from all the other times.

But there is another way of remembering that doesn't rely on cues. Remembering the future in the way I have described is about remembering out-of-the-ordinary events and needs. Remembering to feed the cat isn't usually a problem, because you do it every day. It's part of your routine. Remembering to feed the neighbors' cat when they're away is harder.

We need to distinguish between what might be termed long-term intentions (irregular actions you need to remember to do hours or days or even months in the future), short-term intentions (actions you intend to carry out within a few minutes), and routine actions.

To understand what can go wrong with short-term intentions (that oh-so-familiar situation where you find yourself in a place with no recollection of what you meant to do there), and routine actions, we need to understand two very important systems: **working memory** and attention. In both cases, failures to remember are less failures of memory than they are failures of these systems.

Main points

Your memory deals with different types of information in different ways.

Future actions and events are remembered differently from past events and facts.

Stored information is triggered by appropriate retrieval cues when required.

You cannot rely on the fortuitous appearance of appropriate triggers for the remembrance of intended actions.

Remembering an intention is further complicated by the need to remember it at a specified or an appropriate time.

Short-term goals and short-term memory

Working memory

Working memory governs your ability to comprehend what you are reading or hearing, your ability to learn new words, your ability to reason, your ability to plan and organize yourself, and much more.

Despite its importance, however, it is a relatively recent term, a refinement of an older concept — that of short-term memory. Short-term memory was so named to distinguish it from "long-term memory"— your memory store.

One important difference between short-term memory and working memory, however, is that short-term memory is different from long-term memory chiefly in the *duration* of the records it holds. But working memory, as its name suggests, is something different — it is a process, a state of consciousness.

To put information into our long-term memory store, we must encode it, which generally means we must actively process it — work on it. This we term being "in working memory".

Essentially, being in working memory is a way of saying information is currently being worked on. It's not necessary, by the way, for all of this to be conscious, although mostly it will be.

Similarly, when we're getting information out of the memory store — when we're "remembering" — the information again passes through this state of consciousness, this working memory.

But here we come to the nub of the issue. Our long-term memory store is incredibly large, but the amount we can process at any one time — the amount we can "hold" in working memory — is very very small. Moreover, and very relevantly for our present discussion, you can only keep something "active" for a very short time without your conscious attention. Which is why, if you're trying to remember a phone number long enough to get to a phone and enter it, you have to perform some sort of memory strategy on it (commonly, we simply keep repeating it to ourselves).

Working with information requires us to "hold" it in working memory, which is very small, and requires a deliberate effort.

Working memory capacity and the magic number seven

Probably the most widely known 'fact' about working memory is that it can only hold around seven chunks of information (between 5 and 9). However, this tells us little about the limits of working memory because the size of a chunk is indeterminate.

1 2 3 4 5 6 7 are seven different chunks — if you remember each digit separately (as you would, for example, if you were not familiar with the digits — as a young child isn't). But for those of us who are only too well-versed in our numbers, 1 to 7 could be a single chunk.

In any case, recent research suggests that it is not so much the *number* of chunks that is important, but how long it takes you to say the words (information is usually held in working memory in the form of an acoustic — a sound-based — code). It appears that you can only hold in working memory what you can say in 1.5 — 2 seconds. Slow speakers are therefore penalized! (This also explains why we tend to talk very fast when we have a lot of information we want to disgorge).

Working memory is critical

But what we term "working memory" is not a single entity. It contains several functions, including the "central executive" which coordinates and manages the various tasks needed. The extent to which working memory is domain-specific (different "working memories", if you like, for different sensory and cognitive systems, such as language, spatial memory, number) is still very much debated. However, at a practical level, it is useful to think of working memory as containing several different components, for which you have different "capacities". Thus, your capacity for numbers may well be quite different from your capacity for words, and both from your capacity for visual images.

Although working memory is very small, there is more than one, so you can increase your capacity by using more than one at a time. However, you are also limited by the abilities of your central executive to manage everything.

This is important, because it means you can spread the load among several systems. For example, when I need to remember, say, a phone number and a name, I'll repeat one while holding the other as a visual image — writing the name, as it were, on a mental whiteboard.

> If my wife is talking to me [while driving], although I'll be concentrating on the route, we often miss a turn we should have taken. Yet if a roadside sign or advertisement is passed I can seem to take a snapshot in my mind and recall and 'read' the details after it has been left behind. My wife can only manage to read the first one or two words while it is in view.
>
> Tony, technical writer, 73

Working memory and attention

I said that working memory capacity appears to be limited by how much you can say in 1.5—2 seconds, but that, of course, applies only to verbal working memory. What about other types of working memory, and is there a common measure that applies to all working memory systems?

Recently, a theory of working memory has been developed that posits that working memory capacity reflects the extent to which a person can control attention, particularly in situations where there is competing information / demands. In other words, the undeniable differences between people's working memory capacity is not so much because people differ in how much information they can keep active, but because they vary in their ability to control attention.

The central executive may be thought of as the attention controller, meaning your working memory capacity is affected by your ability to control your attention.

Now this makes a great deal of sense, and ties together two absolutely fundamental concepts: working memory and attention (and links them both to intelligence, but that's a story for another day).

It also suggests an approach for increasing your working memory capacity. But before we can look at that, we need to understand what attention is.

There are two aspects to attention. One is a deliberate and purposeful act, and the other is the purely involuntary capture of our attention by something in the environment, such as a flashing light or unexpected sound. The attention that is under our control acts in two ways: by focusing on particular information, and by ignoring irrelevant information. Both are equally important.

> Attention can be controlled deliberately, or captured involuntarily. Attention is not only about focus, but also about ignoring distraction.

And this is, essentially, what the central executive function of the working memory system is doing — directing attention appropriately. This can be a complex task, depending on how much competing information and how many competing tasks are involved. For example, imagine you're driving a car and talking to a passenger, and then a bird dives right across your windscreen and your cellphone rings, just as your passenger asks you about the state of your unhappy marriage. And all at the same time, you have to decide whether the shape moving in front of you requires you to take action, whether to answer the phone, and what to tell your passenger.

Except we don't do anything "at the same time". Not anything that requires attention, at any rate. We can't split our attention. The best we can do is switch it very, very fast. And there's a cost to that.

> Attention can't be divided.

Switching attention comes at a cost

How big a cost depends on a number of factors. If you are driving a familiar route, with no unexpected events (such as the car in front of you braking hard, or a dog running out on the road), you may not notice the deterioration in your performance when you're talking at the same time. It also helps if the conversation you are having is routine, with little emotional engagement. But if the conversation is stressful, or provokes strong emotion, or requires you to think … well, any of these factors will impact on your ability to drive.

This ability to switch attention between tasks is regulated by the executive control function. Executive control is associated primarily with the **prefrontal cortex**, which is a region of the brain that appears to be particularly affected by aging, and also by alcohol. In other words, as we get older (or more intoxicated!), we become less able to switch attention fast.

> Switching attention takes time. How long it takes depends on the familiarity and complexity of the tasks, and the individual's ability.

But even younger adults don't multitask nearly as well as they think they do. No one is immune to the fact that switching between tasks takes time; the more complex or unfamiliar the tasks, the greater the time.

Part of the problem in switching attention is that we have to change "rules". Rules are what tell us precisely how to process the information in a particular task. Rule activation takes significant amounts of time, several tenths of a second — which may not sound much, but can mean the difference between life and death in some situations (such as driving a car), and which even in less dramatic circumstances adds appreciably to the time it takes to do tasks, if you are switching back and forth repeatedly.

To take an example close to home, people required to write a report while repeatedly checking their email took half again as long to finish the report compared to those who didn't switch between tasks.

It's also been speculated that rapid switching between tasks may impede long-term memory encoding, and a recent study seems to bear that out. The study found that, although immediate learning appeared unaffected when students learned a simple classification task while distracted by another task, brain scans showed a less effective part of the brain was being used, and students later showed they were unable to extrapolate from what they had learned[8].

> I find I can readily focus and put energy into any one job, but two (or more) at a time I find difficult.
>
> Ian, farmer, 51
>
>
> I easily get distracted, if [while doing another task] someone talks to me and asks for another task to be done; either I complete my task and forget theirs or I act on their request and forget what I intended to do
>
> Tony, technical writer, 73

Attention is not a single entity

Another feature of attention is that it probably isn't a single mechanism. Evidence suggests there are several different attention networks, all associated with different parts of the brain, and all competing for control. You can see why the central executive is so important!

The two functions of attention

I said that attention involves what we might think of as a positive process (deliberately keeping certain information active) and a negative one (blocking information that might be distracting).

The idea that the ability to block out irrelevant information is a critical aspect of good attentional control is demonstrated by a recent study.

There are a lot of voices in the brain clamoring for attention — it's the job of your attention controller to decide which to listen to.

There's a classic psychological study, in which people are given two streams of audio, one for each ear, and instructed to listen only to one. At some point, the person's name is spoken into the unattended stream, and about a third of people pick that up. This was dubbed the "cocktail party phenomenon". In a recent take of that study, researchers compared the performance of people as a function of their working memory capacity. Only 20% of those with a high capacity heard their name in the unattended channel compared to 65% of low-capacity people.

A crucial part of controlling attention is deciding what not to listen to. People with a 'higher' working memory capacity are better at ignoring the wrong voices.

In a way this seems paradoxical — you'd think the people with the ability to hold more in working memory would have the resources to spare for additional information. Which is why this finding is so telling. Yes, the higher-capacity people have more resources, but part of how they're using those resources is to filter out information that doesn't matter.

The ability to block out distraction not only varies between people, it is also one that tends to get worse as we age. (In fact, this tendency may be at the heart of many of the problems in cognitive function that we associate with age).

The second problem we have is keeping information active —

which is not nearly as easy as we seem to think. We tend to overestimate how much information we can keep active at one time. Part of the reason for that is that we don't realize how quickly information "falls out" of working memory if we don't engage a deliberate strategy to keep it there.

> I find if the telephone rings and the call is unimportant I immediately forget.
>
> Betty, retired farmer, 81

Indeed, we're inclined to believe that we don't need to do anything to maintain a thought, particularly when it has popped into our minds easily. But current estimates are that unrehearsed information (information we're not actively repeating to ourselves) lingers in working memory for less than two seconds!

So even a very, very short delay between recalling an intention and being able to carry it out is sufficient to dramatically reduce the likelihood that you will remember to do the intended action. Is it any wonder our short-term intentions slip away so often?

Without deliberate effort, we can only keep information active for a couple of seconds.

This problem is also exacerbated by age — and this time I'm not talking about advanced age. This aspect of cognitive processing begins to decline as early as the thirties.

Age and attention

It's important to note that, although age may worsen our ability to block out distraction, it's by no means inevitable. One study[9] of older adults found six of sixteen had no problems.

So why do some older adults have difficulty screening out distractions while others don't? And the burning question, of course — is there anything you can do to make sure you're in the latter group?

Research suggests that the reason lies in the concentration of white matter in the frontal lobes. Brain tissue is made up of two types of material: the "grey matter" of the cell bodies of neurons, and the "white matter" of their axons — the long tails that carry the messages between neurons. Axons are sheathed with a white substance called myelin that makes the signals travel faster (think of the colored plastic insulating electrical wires). While gray matter starts to decline in the twenties, white matter keeps increasing until it starts to decline in the late forties. It is this reduction in white matter, then, that seems to be chiefly reflected in age-related cognitive decline.

> Your ability to control attention may decline with age if you loss too much white matter in the frontal lobes of your brain.

Those whose ability to block out distraction has worsened with age show a dramatic loss of white matter in the frontal lobes[10].

Excitingly, there is probably something you can do to prevent this.

Preventing loss of function

Physical fitness appears to slow this decline. The effects of exercise on cognition in older adults are now well-documented. Clearly, exercise improves cognition through more than one mechanism. But in the present context, we need to note that exercise seems to particularly benefit the frontal lobes, and executive function[11].

> Physical exercise can counteract this decline.

Exercise also seems to benefit older women more than older men[12], and those on hormone therapy more than other post-menopausal women[13]. Interestingly, women tend to have more developed frontal lobes (more neurons) than men, but as if to even the score, women appear to lose cells faster from this area as they age[14]. Perhaps this is the reason why women benefit more from strategies that counteract neuron loss.

So what sort of exercise should you do? Research suggests exercise that incorporates both aerobic exercise (such as brisk walking) and strength training is most effective, and doing it for longer than 30 minutes at a time.

What you need to know about working memory

The amount of information we can "hold" in working memory is very very small.

It appears that you can only hold in working memory what you can say in 1.5 — 2 seconds, so talking fast helps.

Working memory contains different systems, including a "central executive" which coordinates everything. You can increase your functional capacity by using more than one system.

Working memory capacity may reflect the extent to which a person can control attention, particularly in situations where there is competing information / demands.

What you need to know about attention

Attention can be deliberately focused or captured involuntarily.

Attention can't be divided; when we're doing more than one task, we're really switching attention very, very fast.

Switching takes longer the more complex or unfamiliar the tasks.

Blocking out irrelevant information is a critical aspect of good attentional control. People with 'high' working memory capacity appear to be better at blocking irrelevant information.

Keeping information active is harder than we think. Without a deliberate strategy to keep it active (such as repeating the information), information can probably only stay active for less than two seconds.

The ability to keep information active without intervention begins to decline in our thirties.

The ability to switch attention often (but not always) worsens with more advanced age.

The ability to block out distraction also tends to get worse with more advanced age.

Those who have difficulty screening out distractions seem to have less white matter in the frontal lobes.

Physical exercise seems to be of particular benefit for slowing this loss, especially for women.

Forgetting what you're doing

Working memory, therefore, has to not only keep a tight hold of information relevant to our goals ("I'm going to the study to get a stapler"), it also has to inhibit our responses to information that might distract us from our goal (seeing a book you were looking for earlier; remembering you were going to ring someone).

We've talked about how this capacity is affected by our ability to control attention:

- that attention can only focus on one thing at a time;
- that attention can be captured by things in the environment (which includes our own mind — sometimes we're captured by our own thoughts);
- that the more complex, or the more unfamiliar, the task, the slower we are to switch attention;
- that our ability to switch attention, and our ability to block out distracting information (which might be seen as our ability to resist capture) often gets worse with age; and
- how quickly information is lost from working memory if we make no effort to keep it there.

Now let's see how all that applies to the real-life memory failures and absent-minded errors we make every day.

Short-term memory problems are attention problems

Many people, particularly as they get older, have concerns about short-term memory problems:

- going to another room to do something and then forgetting why you're there;
- deciding to do something, becoming distracted by another task, and then forgetting the original intention;
- being uncertain about whether you have just performed a routine task;
- forgetting things you've said or done seconds after having said or done them;
- thinking of something you want to say during a conversation, then forgetting what it was by the time it's your turn to speak,

and so on.

Well, after reading the previous chapter, you can see why these problems often become worse with age, and also, I hope, you can see why these are not, strictly speaking, failures of memory.

When we get in our car to drive to place A and find ourselves instead on the road to the more familiar place B, this is not a failure of memory. When we clear the table and find ourselves putting the margarine in the dishwasher or the dirty plate in the fridge, this is not a failure of memory. When we go into a room intending to do one thing and do something else instead, this is not, really, a failure of memory.

These are failures of attention.

They are absentminded errors, and they happen to all of us. For example, a study involving around a hundred people at two research organizations found that of the 182 "memory problems" mentioned, just under a quarter were **action slips**[15].

The term 'action slips' is useful because it points more precisely to the nature of these errors.

Action slips include such types of error as:

- actions you've forgotten doing, such as going to lock the door after you've already locked it, or taking pills twice

- substituted actions, such as putting the butter in the dishwasher, or driving in a familiar direction instead of the required one

place-losing errors, where you've lost your "place" in an action sequence, and so omit or repeat part of the sequence (for example, if distracted while baking to a familiar recipe, you may be unsure where you are in the sequence, and omit or repeat an ingredient)

- blends, where you get confused between two active tasks (for example, you write an email while thinking about the next email you're going to write, and address the current email to the correspondent for the second email)

- reversals, where you get confused between parts of the same task (for example, you put an empty ice cube tray in the freezer, then turn to the tap to fill it)

- discrimination errors, such as mistaking yogurt for milk, or a magazine for a book.

None of these are really caused by memory failure as such. Clearly you know what you *should* be doing as soon as you notice what you *are* doing.

The first type of error — doing things twice, or simply wondering if you've done something — while it does seem to be more of a memory failure than the others, is however, like the others, a failure of attention, not memory. All of these occur only when the action is part of your habitual routine, and they occur because we pay little attention to our habitual routine.

> Making errors in tasks because you forget what you're doing or what you've done is a failure of attention, not memory.

You can also see from all this that these everyday errors occur in the context of action sequences — that is, sequences of actions that we have practiced so often they have become automatic. Dressing, undressing, washing, making coffee or tea, even making quite complicated recipes (if familiar enough) — these are all common examples of action sequences.

So let's look at action sequences.

Action sequences are why we make action slips

Action slips are so common because much of what we do every day concerns familiar, well-practiced actions. Actions like getting dressed, cleaning our teeth, making breakfast, walking from one particular place to another, driving a car, locking the house ... The list goes on and on. When these things were new — when we were acquiring these skills and patterns of behavior —

we had to think about them. But with practice, they became automatic. Mature adults spend a lot of their day on auto-pilot!

Action slips become more frequent as actions become more automatized. Unlike other errors, they are therefore signs of expertise.

> Action slips are signs of expertise, so it's not surprising they become more common with age!

Actions are not self-contained. A sustained action sequence such as making coffee or getting dressed is made up of a number of elements, some of which will also be used by other action sequences (which also explains why action slips become more common with age — as we get older, more of our actions are very well-practiced).

For example, making instant coffee might involve:

- getting a mug
- getting the coffee from wherever it's kept
- opening the jar/packet
- getting a spoon
- spooning the right amount of coffee into the mug
- putting water in a kettle/jug to boil
- turning on the kettle/jug
- getting milk out of the fridge
- getting the sugar from wherever it's kept
- waiting for the water to boil
- pouring the water into the mug
- stirring it
- adding sugar

- adding milk

Action slips occur because action sequences are made up of common elements.

This all seems very pedantic, but there it is — even a simple action sequence like this is composed of lots of very simple actions. Think about them, and note how many will be used by other action sequences.

The most obvious is making tea, but action elements such as getting out a spoon, getting sugar, getting milk, are all involved in a number of other action sequences. Whether you ever get them confused depends entirely on whether you employ such action sequences on a regular basis.

For example, if you put milk and sugar on your morning cereal, this might easily, in moments of distraction, get confused with your coffee-making. Particularly if time and place are the same.

Vulnerable points in the sequence

Action slips tend to occur at points in the sequence which are preceded by actions or objects that are associated with different actions — these are called branch points or decision points. For example, Reason[16] tells us how "I meant to get my car out, but as I passed the back porch on the way to the garage I stopped to put on my boots and gardening jacket as if to work in the yard."

Lapsing from one action to another like this has been, very suitably, termed **capture** — a phenomenon we're already familiar with. Capture tends to happen, naturally enough, after a series of actions shared by both tasks.

Thus, the other day I went to the basement to get a saw, but opened the freezer instead (the secondary freezer we keep in the basement being the reason for me to go down there nine times out of ten). In the same vein, one researcher[17] refers to an occasion when, shortly after playing cards, he was photocopying some papers and found himself counting, '1, 2, 3, 4, 5, 6, 7, 8, 9, 10, Jack, Queen, King', and a nineteenth-century researcher[18] describes how very absentminded people have gone to their bedroom to dress for dinner, and instead changed into their nightclothes and gone to bed.

> Sequences are more vulnerable to derailment at the junctions between subroutines.

The idea of decision points reflects an idea that well-learned action sequences consist of highly practiced subsequences that don't require close attention, but that the points at which these subroutines join (the decision points) does require attention — hence their apparent vulnerability to distraction.

This seems plausible. Decision points are not simply transitions between subroutines, but points where you have to make a decision about what the next action will be — a decision that requires information about the preceding actions and the broader context. For example, at the point of adding sugar to the coffee, you must decide whether you've already done it (for sugar may be added at more than one point in the sequence) and whether it's wanted (perhaps you're making coffee for someone else, or you only allow yourself sugar sometimes).

> Although sequences may go awry at junctions between subroutines, the culprit may be inattention in the middle of the subroutine, not at the junction itself.

Now certainly the transitions from one subroutine to another are the points where action sequences are most likely to fail, but a newer theory suggests that it is not distraction at the decision point that causes these, but distraction occurring around the *middle* of the previous subroutine[19].

This theory (which is supported by a detailed mechanism for how action sequences are produced) suggests that action slips occur because the mental representation is not clearly specified. This point has also been emphasized by other researchers — as has the corollary that, when the idea in your head isn't sufficiently well specified, your actions will tend to default to actions that are high-frequency and appropriate for the context.

In other words, when you're not clear in your head about what you're doing, you'll tend to default to related, familiar actions.

According to this new model, however, errors occur at decision points not so much because your intention wasn't clear enough in the first place, but because your mental representation has become degraded — something that is most likely to occur because of distraction at a crucial earlier time. For example, if your attention was distracted (due to some outside event such as someone talking to you, or some internal preoccupation as a thought occurs to you) while you were adding sugar at an earlier point in the sequence, then when you come to decide whether you need to add sugar, the information that you've done it is no longer there.

> The most common type of action slip is mainly caused by distraction during a subroutine.

The model suggests that while differences in contexts are strongly represented at decision points (as you'd expect, since these are where you need the information most), distinctions between different contexts are represented less strongly in the middle of subroutines (where, after all, habit is controlling the production of actions). This, of course, makes it easier for the system's representation of context to become disrupted at this point.

To go back to our coffee-making example: to know whether to add the sugar after adding cream, you need to have kept safe the information that you have (or haven't) added sugar *before* adding cream for the whole time that you are adding cream. Now that, of course, isn't a long time, but remember how quickly information can be lost if we make no effort to hold onto it. The fact that the information is not immediately relevant (you are going to add cream regardless of what you do with the sugar) makes the information more vulnerable to loss.

Of course, the mental representation will be more vulnerable if there are very similar contexts. Think of your mental representation as a sketchy drawing. If the drawing (having lost some of the detail that would make it unique) could easily represent more than one situation, then you're going to choose the one that's most likely, aren't you? You're going to choose the highest-frequency possibility from recent history. Which is why, cut adrift for the moment from my intention to get the saw, I defaulted to the freezer.

Common types of action slip

In the most extensive study of absentminded errors, involving a diary study in which 35 volunteers noted their action slips over two weeks and an extended diary study in which 63 students recorded their action slips in much greater detail over a week, James Reason collected 625 action slips and classified the vast majority — 88% — as belonging to one of four types:

Repetition: an action is unnecessarily repeated (for example, putting sugar into your tea twice).

Omission: an action is omitted (for example, forgetting to put the yeast in your bread dough — that's a favorite of mine! Or writing out a check, then putting the checkbook away without tearing out the check.).

Intrusion: an action from another action sequence

inappropriately intrudes (such as calling "come in" when you answer the phone).

Object confusion: the wrong object is used (for example, taking the cheese out of the fridge instead of the margarine).

Intrusions seem to be the most common (or perhaps the most noticeable). The detailed diary study revealed that 40% of the 192 slips were intrusions.

This is supported by a more recent questionnaire of 85 employees in two research organizations. This found that by far the most common types of action slips were:

- carrying out an intention that wasn't intended (as in our example of dressing for bed rather than dinner), and

- carrying out an unnecessary action (such as reaching to take off your glasses when you're not wearing them).

Repetitions, omissions, and intrusions, might all be thought of as **sequencing errors**. Sequencing errors also include reversals (when we mix up the sequence) and anticipation errors (moving on to a subroutine before a necessary earlier subroutine is completed).

We can get a better grasp of why these errors happen by going back to our action model.

Intrusions mostly happen for the reason we've just talked about — because our attention is captured at decision points in the sequence when our mental representation of what we're doing has become degraded (generally because of distraction prior to the decision point).

Repetition errors tend to occur in action sequences that involve elements that are commonly repeated — which is why you are more likely to make a mistake putting in too many spoonfuls of coffee or sugar, than in repeatedly filling the kettle with water.

This makes sense if you think of action sequences as involving not only elements, but also rules. Think about it — if action sequences are made up of common elements, how does your processor know which ones to take and when, for any particular sequence?

So some elements will have rules attached that allow for repetitions, and others will be set up to move on to the next element as soon as they're executed. Elements that have repetition rules attached are obviously much more likely to produce repetition errors. Moreover, the more often you actually repeat the action, the more likely you are to fall victim to a repetition error. Thus, if you habitually make coffee for you and another, you are much more likely to get out two mugs when you are drinking alone, than someone who generally only makes a drink for herself.

Omissions can involve simply missing out a step (perhaps, but not necessarily, after an interruption), or the omission of a step or steps because you have moved on to the next activity prematurely — as when you walk out of a shop without waiting for your change. Omissions result from skipping a subroutine.

Object confusion

Using the wrong object is obviously a different type of error to the sequencing errors we've been considering. And yet, it may not be as different as it seems. Objects are clearly important triggers of action sequences. Indeed, we tend to categorize objects on the basis of similarities not between the objects themselves, but between the actions they invite.

The model takes the very plausible view that object selection and action selection are very similar processes. This explains why action slips often begin with mistakes in object selection.

Object confusion can occur not only because our mental plan has degraded and left us subject to capture by familiar objects. It can also begin with a simple perceptual failure. We mistake one object for another because we are not looking closely and the two objects are similar. In such a case, we're likely to choose the more familiar or the more expected object. We tend to see what we expect to see.

This can even occur when we *are* paying attention, if we can't see it clearly enough. Again, in the case of ambiguity, we default to the most likely — a complex calculation based not only on appearance, but also on context, recency, and familiarity. Interestingly, it's been suggested that we are particularly likely to suffer this type of perceptual failure immediately after some highly stressful event, as we relax our vigilance.

> Apart from sequencing errors of one kind or other, the other main class of action slip occurs because we mistake an object for another, usually more familiar, object. This can be an attention or a perceptual failure.

It's also worth noting that we are often extremely reluctant to give up such false impressions, even as the evidence mounts that we have made a mistake.

Situations when action slips are most likely

On the basis of his extensive study of absent-minded errors,

Reason identified three conditions that promote this type of error:

Well-established or routine sequence of actions that are largely automatized, and in which the demands upon continuous attention are relatively small.

Being distracted or preoccupied — specifically, being in a state when your limited attentional resource is allocated to something unrelated to the activity.

A relatively familiar environment where there are few departures from the expected, and thus little vigilance is required.

He noted that in the case of the most common type of error — intrusions — the intruding activity was consistently one that was recently and frequently engaged in, and one sharing similar locations, movements, and objects (sometimes, but less often, timing and/or purpose).

> Action slips generally occur when you are engaged in a routine activity in a familiar place while preoccupied.

It was also likely that one of the following provoking factors was present:

Entering a familiar environment with your mind in a "reduced state of intentionality" — that is, your purpose is not in the forefront of your mind.

Something, perhaps a change in goal, has altered a well-established routine — such as when you decide to give up putting sugar in your coffee, and find yourself doing it anyway.

Something has changed in your familiar environment, necessitating a change in your routine — such as when you move an article of furniture, and find yourself constantly going to the wrong place.

Something in the environment you're in shares many common elements with a very familiar context — for example, standing at a friend's door trying to open it with your own key.

Interestingly, being distressed, physically unwell, or in a hurry, weren't particularly important factors, although fatigue sometimes was. Later research has suggested boredom can also be a factor[20]. But it was simple preoccupation or distraction that underscored most action slips.

It's also worth noting that there was a time of day effect. Action slips were fewer in the early afternoon (between noon and 3pm), and then rose again, to peak between 5 and 7pm. This early evening peak appears to reflect the fact that it's time to prepare the evening meal — the kitchen is a favorite place for absent-minded errors.

The kitchen is a prime place for many of us to make action slips because it is a familiar environment which is associated with many overlearned action sequences — sequences, moreover, which tend to share common elements. Realizing that, you should readily be able to think of the places in which you are most vulnerable to errors of this kind.

Characteristics of action slips

Action slips:

- usually occur during the performance of tasks that are so highly practiced they are largely automatic.
- usually occur when we are preoccupied or distracted.
- often involve intrusions of other habitual actions that share some characteristics with the intended action.

Such habit intrusions are more likely to occur when:

- we're departing in some way from our usual routine (for example, you decide to stop adding milk and sugar to your coffee, then finding yourself doing it automatically)
- the situation has changed, demanding a change in our usual routine (for example, a much-visited shop moves premises, but you keep going to its old location)
- the situation shares features with a highly familiar situation (for example, you try and open a friend's car with your own car key)

Have I done it already?

> Cleaning my teeth after washing in the bathroom, I often have to feel the bristles of the toothbrush to see if I actually did clean my teeth
>
> Tony, technical writer, 73

A complication of successful remembering of intentions that may particularly affect older adults is that sometimes you are uncertain as to whether or not you have already carried out the intention. Taking medication is a prime example. So are household tasks. Did I already take my pill, or not? Did I turn the water-heating off? Did I put the beans on to soak?

A large part of the problem is that these are regular acts, occurring in the same contexts over and over again. You always take your pill with juice at breakfast? Well, did you do it this morning?

Hard to answer. The memory of doing it is familiar, but what's to distinguish your memory of this morning from your memory of yesterday morning?

It is not only the frequency and indistinguishability of repeated occurrences that can cause confusion. If, when you are reminding yourself to perform some action later, you visualize yourself doing it, it can be hard, later on, to distinguish between the memory of your imagined vision, and a memory of actually performing the act. (Our difficulty in telling apart "real" memories and imagined events is indeed one of the particularly fascinating aspects of memory!)

This aspect of remembering — knowing whether in fact something has happened — has been termed reality-monitoring, and there is some evidence that older adults may be less effective at it than younger adults[21]. This may be related to loss of source memory — older adults are more likely than younger people to not fully encode context information, meaning that they are less sure where and when something happened.

Although habitual acts are easier to remember to do, it is harder to remember whether you have already performed the action. This seems to be particularly difficult for older adults.

The situation is complicated by the fact that such errors aren't solely caused by a lack of attention. They can also be caused by too much attention.

Or perhaps it is truer to say that it's all about applying the right amount of attention at the right time. We're all familiar with the way too much attention can disturb a largely automatic sequence. Checking on the progress of a habitual task at the wrong time can also disturb the flow, particularly if a quick visual check is not guaranteed to give the right answer (for example, looking at your cup of coffee will tell you if you've put cream in, but not whether you've added sugar).

It also seems that we use unresolved tension as part of this system. The tension is a by-product of our monitoring system. Think again of our action sequence model. Imagine an inspector ticking off each element as it's completed. But what happens if he misses a tick? You're left with the feeling that there's something you've forgotten.

You can see that this is very like what happens with repetition errors, suggesting that actions that are repeated will be especially prone to this error. Common problems such as being unsure whether you've locked the house, or turned off the power, when going away on holiday, may result from a repetition in this particular context — although you only perform these actions once, you may be in the habit of checking your action. If you miss out this check (which might simply be a verbal note to yourself that you've done it), you'll be left with the feeling that you've missed something.

What makes some people more prone to absent-minded errors?

There is no doubt that some people are more prone to these types of errors than others. One reason might be that they have more attentional demands on them. These demands might be caused by intellectual thought (the absent-minded professor is a stock figure, although research has found no correlation between the tendency to make these kinds of errors and test intelligence or educational attainment[22]), or emotional distress.

As I have already mentioned, emotion appears to be particularly distracting. Brain imaging studies have shown that emotional information and attentional functions travel parallel paths in the brain and then meet up in an area between the frontal lobes. Since this area is thought to be critically involved in deciding where attention should be directed, it is not surprising that emotion should be particularly distracting. And perhaps this is one reason why some people are more easily distracted than others — they are more affected by emotion[23].

There is some evidence that people who are vulnerable to stress may be more likely to be error-prone[24].

Perhaps this is because part of working memory is taken up with our awareness of fears and worries, leaving less capacity

Anxious people may be more prone to absent-minded errors, because some of their attention is taken up with their anxiety.

available for processing. In support of this theory, one study found that math-anxious people have working memory problems as they do math.

And perhaps the popular association between pregnancy and mental fogginess, absent-mindedness, and forgetfulness, is related to increased anxiety. Is this association a myth, or is there some justification for this belief?

In general, studies have found some justification for this belief, with estimates ranging from 50% to 80% of pregnant women feeling that they have experienced some decline in cognitive function[25]. But evidence suggests that the main culprit is probably the change in sleep patterns[26, 27].

Sleep deprivation certainly affects working memory — we all know that from personal experience! It has also been confirmed by research. Sleep-deprived people have not only been shown to perform an arithmetic task involving working memory more poorly, brain scans have confirmed less activity in the prefrontal cortex[28]. Sleep-deprived participants have also showed poorer performance in a task where they have to divide their attention[29].

Lack of sleep also reduces working memory capacity, which may be why we make more absent-minded errors when tired.

But it's not all about the demands of attention. Remember, a lot of the problem of attentional control has to do with the ability to block out distraction. And people clearly differ in this ability.

A study using an eye-tracking task found that relatively error-prone people made significantly more unintended, stimulus-driven eye movements[30]. (Our eyes are constantly in motion, although we are rarely aware of it — a mechanism in our brain cleverly provides the illusion of stability). By stimulus-driven, we mean that something in the environment attracts the wandering eye.

The findings support the idea that some people are more susceptible to being captured by environmental cues, which then trigger actions that they hadn't intended. For example, when I went down to the basement, as I opened the door, my eye was caught by a well-developed cobweb next to the freezer. The sight distracted my thoughts, erasing the intention I had come with, and then my wandering eye next lit upon the neighboring freezer — a familiar object associated with a very familiar action — and I opened it.

A twin study suggests that a large part of what determines whether an individual is prone to absent-mindedness errors is genetic[31]. In other words, the tendency runs in families.

> Some people are more easily distracted — and this might be genetic.

There is also some evidence that dyslexics are more vulnerable to such problems, apparently being more easily distracted, and also having a tendency to over-focus, so that relevant peripheral information is missed[32].

And, of course, as we've already discussed, aging is also commonly associated with increased absentmindedness. However, although older adults are more susceptible to particular kinds or error — in particular, those that stem from losing track of previous events — there is no direct evidence that older people are more prone to absentmindedness in general[33]. This may be because older adults are more inclined than younger people to employ strategies to counter such errors.

How to prevent action slips

Is there anything we can do to minimize action slips?

There are two parts to the answer to this question: general

strategies for improving your attentional control, and specific strategies for particular situations.

Let's start by noting that telling yourself (or other people) to pay attention is not enough! It's like a teacher telling students to take notes without making sure they know how to do so effectively. And paying attention is not something that anyone trains us to do — partly because it's assumed that we all know what "paying attention" means, and mostly because we don't really understand how we pay attention.

> Last week I experienced inattention that surprised me. We were eating out at a place that had lots of photos of celebrities on the walls — sportspeople, entertainers, politicians — and I noticed that they all seemed to have short Asian partners without realizing that these were the same woman, the proprietor of the business.
>
> Robin

Attention is probably most easily studied in terms of perception, as in a visual search task (think of the "I spy"-type games and books we give children). An interesting study looked at the best way to train people whose jobs require them to identify objects or patterns in a visual display (such as air traffic controllers). The study found that those who started their training on relatively clear, uncluttered displays learned more quickly, and transferred their learning to cluttered displays as soon as they were given them. However, those who started on cluttered displays didn't show any transferred improvement when given clear displays.

> One way to improve your attentional control is to practice searching visual displays.

The study not only points to the best way to improve your visual search abilities, it also underscores the independence of these two mechanisms: the process of focusing, and the process of filtering out distraction.

Does this apply beyond perceptual learning? It may be that it reflects a more general principle: that if you want to improve your attentional control, you should approach these two functions separately. And that you would be better to begin by training yourself to focus before tackling blocking[34].

Another perceptual study[35] has examined the phenomenon called "perceptual rivalry", which arises when different images are presented to each eye and the two fight for domination of the image to be perceived. Although this might be thought of as an automatic process, perceptual rivalry is nevertheless thought to involve those attentional mechanisms we've been talking about.

The study involved 76 Tibetan Buddhist monks trained in meditation. During a practice known as "one-point" meditation, described as the maintained focus of attention on a single object or thought, perceptual rivalry was significantly altered, with longer periods of perceptual dominance seen in those monks practicing one-point meditation. Indeed, three of the more experienced monks were able to maintain a stable image for the entire five-minute period. This effect was not seen in those practicing "compassion"-oriented meditation, described as a contemplation of suffering within the world combined with an emanation of loving kindness.

Even when not engaged in meditation, stable perception was longer among the monks (4.1 seconds) than among control subjects who were not experienced in meditation (2.6 seconds). In fact, one monk was able to maintain a constant image for over 12 minutes!

> Meditation is another strategy for improving your attentional control.

The findings not only point to a way of

training attention, but also demonstrate that even apparently automatic sensory processes can be controlled.

There is some evidence that ignoring distraction is in fact much easier when you're engaged in tasks that are highly perceptual (for example, searching a heap of multi-colored jelly beans for the green ones), and much harder when you're engaged in a highly cognitive task (such as writing a book!)$_{36}$. Another reason to start with perceptual tasks.

A program for improving attentional control and reducing absentminded errors

There are three parts to such a program. The first part applies to those who feel that their abilities have been compromised by age, or physical stress (such as caused by obesity or prolonged poor sleep), or mental stress (such as anxiety). Exercise is the most important remedy here, for apart from its direct effect on neurons, it may also improve sleep and even reduce stress.

A healthy diet is also recommended. The evidence is quite clear now that a diet high in antioxidants is good for the brain — that means eating lots of fruit and vegetables, with red-through-black berries especially recommended. It also seems clear that a high-fat diet is bad. Cut back on the high-fat foods and up your intake of low-glycemic carbohydrates (like brown rice) and omega-3 oils (which you can get partly from oily fish, but probably not enough; I put a generous helping of flaxseed oil on my daily salad). But be warned: watch that cutting back on high-fat foods doesn't make you reduce protein to too low a level — research suggests older adults tend not to get enough protein.

It's also recommended that you eat small meals regularly, rather than fewer, bigger meals. This is better for keeping glucose levels stable.

And finally, relaxation techniques are recommended for those suffering from poor sleep or stress. This relaxation could of course involve a meditational technique, thus killing two birds with one stone!

Which leads us to the second part of the program — improving your attentional control. This might involve practicing a meditational technique, or perhaps a physical activity sharing meditational qualities, such as t'ai ch'i or archery (although any effect this may have is speculative). It also might involve activities designed to improve what we might term environmental attentiveness: visual search tasks of various kinds. There are programs online, such as at lumosity.com, which can help you with this.

Finally, the third part concerns specific circumstances. This requires you to think about the particular instances of absentmindedness you are prone to, and be aware of the circumstances that set you up for such errors. Then you can either:

- make a sterling effort to pay attention when it's important to you (for example, both my partner and I are careful when we are driving and need to depart from familiar routes, to remind ourselves of our destination at key points), or
- use an object to signal that you have done something, or remind you where you are in a sequence (to take the recipe example again, you could move used ingredients to a particular part of the kitchen bench), or
- decide it's not important!

Let me give you some examples of specific strategies.

Every morning, I begin the day with two glasses of warm water with lemon juice. Remembering to have these is no problem, as it is a part of my regular routine. Where I come unstuck is knowing whether I've had *both* glasses, or only one. So what I make sure I do, is to remove the squeezed lemon from the bench as soon as I've used it the second time. That way, if I'm uncertain whether I've had both glasses or only one, I simply have to look at the customary place on the bench and see if the lemon is there. If it is, I haven't had my second glass; if it isn't, I have.

I do the same sort of thing when I wash my hair. Because I tend to be lost in thought in the shower, I always make sure I put the shampoo bottle down in one particular, different, place when I've used it the first time, and back in its usual place when I've finished with it. Otherwise, I sometimes lose track, and can't remember whether I've washed my hair twice, or only once.

And here are a couple of strategies told to me by a young mother:

- Putting a rubber band on the wrist when breastfeeding and moving to the other hand to indicate which side is to be started on next feed.
- When sewing and using an iron when needed, using a double adapter with a lamp on the other outlet to show that the iron is switched on.

Specific strategies for particular problems can be very simple, and indeed need to be, because their success depends on you incorporating them into your routine. They are usually easily thought of; the trick is stopping to think!

Steps to Success

Recognize the action sequences you have problems with.

Devise simple actions which will counter the problem (these actions can be as simple as a verbal reminder at a particular point in the sequence).

Make an effort to train yourself to incorporate this action into your sequence, until it has become habitual.

Main points

Habitual actions are particularly vulnerable to confusion about whether you have already done them.

Several factors can make failures of attention more likely:

- Emotion
- Lack of sleep
- Being easily distracted
- Alcohol or drugs

To minimize action slips, you need to improve your attentional control, and devise specific strategies for common situations where you are vulnerable to such slips.

To improve attentional control, you need to:

- improve your physical well-being, where physical factors are likely to be impairing your cognitive function;
- improve your ability to focus, and your ability to filter out distraction.

Structuring your goals

Although remembering long-term intentions is quite a different process to that of remembering what you're doing or just about to do, attention and working memory are relevant to this process too.

And there's something else that we haven't yet discussed, that's also relevant to both. Long-term and short-term intentions are both *goals*. Goals are the driving force of human behavior; goals, it is believed, provide the organizing structure for all that we do.

A hierarchy of goals

Part of the problem of remembering intentions over time is that we are usually holding in memory lots of intentions, with a variety of characteristics.

For example, as the primary caregiver of a family, at almost any time I have a shopping list going. This might start as soon as I leave the supermarket, with the vexed "I forgot to get rice! I'll have to get it next time", and accumulates as time goes on and more items are added to the list (which may be a mental or a physical list). In addition, I will have a whole host of short-term and long-term intentions, some of them involving only myself, others involving family members, friends, or people I work with.

Here's a list of goals from a woman in her 40s:

Today:

- Get something for dinner
- Return DVD

This week:

- Finish report
- Get email inbox down to five

Next few weeks:

- Start planning Christmas
- Have bone density scanned
- Find a new hairdresser
- Make appointment for dental check-up

Long-term goals:

- Lose 20lb
- Start weight training
- Get regular exercise
- Learn Spanish
- Improve son's diet

Here's a list from a man in his eighties:

Tonight:

- put rubbish out

Tomorrow:

- Get drinks etc for the Church youth group.
- Take patient to oncology.

Tomorrow or next day:

- Concreting to do.
- Ring meals on wheels re not being available next time.

Sometime:

- Arrange couples to go on the end of year Friday lunch group overnight trip.
- Write to Lions Club resigning membership.

This sample shows how, at any one time, we have several categories of goals (personal goals; work goals; goals that involve other people); goals that are very specific (*Get something for dinner*) and goals that are quite unspecific (*Get regular exercise*); and goals with different time-periods (today; this week; sometime).

And somehow we keep track of them all! But it doesn't come without effort.

Goals include:

- activities that must occur at specified times
- activities that simply must be done "sometime"
- activities that are required almost every day
- activities that include a number of sub-tasks
- activities that are themselves part of a larger goal
- activities that vary in importance
- activities that involve others

Ordering your goals

To keep track of all these plans we need some way of organizing them. People use various strategies to order the many goals they have in memory. Common prioritizing rules include:

- achieve the most important goals first
- achieve goals that have approaching deadlines
- cluster goals that are geographically close.

Flexibility in ordering

But order is not a fixed attribute. Order changes as circumstances change — for example, if you suddenly realize that an unimportant goal can be accomplished in a place you're in or near, you will usually stop and do it then and there.

There's no problem with goals accomplished ahead of schedule, but what about the converse? Often you intend to perform a task in a particular place or at a particular time, only to find that circumstances are against you (you might go to the bank and find it closed for staff training, for example). In such circumstances, the intention may well drop way down your priority list, to the extent of being almost completely forgotten.

> When circumstances change, intentions are more likely to be forgotten.

For example, making an appointment at the dentist for my older son had the corollary *arrange for my younger son to go to a friend at that time*. But when I made the dentist appointment for my son, it seemed a bad time of day to phone the mother of my other son's friend. And then, of course, I forgot to ring her later. As a general rule, if I can't accomplish a particular task at the time I think of it, I make a note of it, or arrange for some other environmental cue. In this case, however, the cue was for the appointment itself (a note on the calendar), not for this related arrangement. The note on the calendar works fine for the appointment, in that I am sure to notice it there in the immediately preceding days, and on the day itself. But by then it might be too late to arrange for my son to play with a friend.

The problem of suspended intentions

It's particularly important in the case of suspended intentions that you give some thought to re-scheduling. Because they are already in memory, it's easy to assume that you will remember them again. However, the very fact that they *are* in memory may well hinder their later recall. Because the information you have stored may now be wrong.

For example, say you intended to use your lunch-break to post a parcel, visit the bank, and buy some stationery. You intend to buy the stationery at the post office. However, when you go there, you discover they don't have the actual stationery you need. There's no other stationery supplier nearby, so you leave it for the moment. *I'll do it some other time*, you promise yourself. And promptly forget about it.

When you formed the intention *get stationery*, you linked it to *post office*, which was linked with *post parcel*. But the parcel has been posted now, and you have no reason to visit the post office. Even passing a book and stationery shop may not remind you of your intention, because the intention was linked to *post office*, not *place that sells stationery*. Depending on how urgent the need for stationery

> When an intention is postponed, you may need to form new memory links.

actually is, the intention may lie dormant in your mind for some time. Until its need becomes more urgent, or you are actually faced with the particular type of stationery you require, or until you once again have a need to go to the post office, and think, "now, wasn't there something else I had to do here?" — the situation triggering an intention that might, now, be weeks old.

What it comes down to is thinking *how* you're going to achieve your goal — making if-then plans, laying out how, where, and when, you'll undertake the actions that will lead to realizing your intention. Such plans are called implementation plans, and research has shown that the better thought-out they are, the more likely you are to achieve your goal.

Implementation plans

Implementation plans don't only specify the behaviors and situations that will help you achieve your goal. Good ones will also specify any situations and behaviors that will stand in the way of you accomplishing your goal. For example, you might specify that you shouldn't keep checking your emails throughout the day (specify particular times or occasions to do it instead, so that you don't keep breaking your current task), or instruct yourself to have an apple when everyone else is having pastries at morning tea.

Implementation plans are particularly important when the task is something that's unpleasant or difficult. One study, for example, found that 92% of women who formed detailed plans on how they would make an appointment for cervical cancer screening did actually get screened, compared to 69% of women who didn't make such plans[37].

There is also evidence that implementation plans are particularly helpful for those with frontal lobe problems, such as schizophrenics and drug addicts — and presumably older adults (although I'm certainly not saying the frontal lobe function of older adults is on a par with these groups!).

Unsurprisingly, implementation plans are most useful when the task is complex — for example, following a medication regimen involving a number of different drugs that require different rules, or preparing a meal involving several different dishes requiring attention at various times.

Implementation plans are thought to be so helpful because they make the situation in which the desired behavior should occur more salient — that is, you'll be more inclined to notice it. It's also thought that specifying the behavior that should occur when confronted by a particular situational cue helps it become automatic. For example, training yourself to automatically go to the stairs when you see the elevator.

Obviously, responding automatically in a particular way to a particular cue will greatly improve your chances of achieving your goal.

The situational cue — the *if* part of the plan — doesn't have to be an external cue in the environment; it can be something internal, like a thought or feeling. Similarly, the behavior — the *then* part of the plan — can be something cognitive, such as a thought. For example, *if I think of having some chocolate, then I'll think of the dress I want to fit into on my birthday*. This can help with increasing motivation — something particularly helpful in the case of long-term goals.

The problem with interruptions

Interruptions might be considered a special type of suspended intention situation. There are two main problems with being interrupted in the course of carrying out an intended task. The first is that the interruption often leads on to another series of tasks, thus taking you further and further away from what you were originally doing, and most importantly, not clearly delineating the end of the interruption. The second is that interruptions are often abrupt and unexpected.

The problem with that is that you don't think about the need to re-code your intention. Again, it's all about re-framing. You need to remind yourself of the need to resume your interrupted task later, and you need to provide some sort of cue that will remind you at the end of the interruption.

You also need to get into the habit of pausing at the end of tasks, to check whether you've finished with all your recent tasks.

Main points

Intentions come in varying types:

- activities that must occur at specified times
- activities that need to be accomplished "some time"
- activities that need to be done regularly
- activities that include a number of sub-tasks
- activities that are themselves part of a larger goal
- activities that vary in importance
- activities that involve others.

Different types of intention require different strategies.

Intentions that have to be postponed may need to be re-framed in memory, with new links.

To remember well, you need to learn how to build effective memory codes.

Circumstances that affect your remembering

How successful you are in remembering intentions is governed most of all by the strategies you use to help you remember, but it is also governed by various circumstances of the particular memory task. The following factors have been suggested as being of some importance$_{38}$:

- the cues that are available (or not available!) to trigger your remembering
- the activity you are engaged in at the time you need to remember the intention
- whether the intended activity is one you have set yourself, or whether it has been imposed by others
- how important it is to you
- whether it involves other people, or only yourself
- whether exact timing is required
- how complex the task is (does it involve only one action, or a series of actions?)

Event-based retrieval cues are better than time-based

I said earlier that remembering in general occurs in response to some cue or trigger, and that one of the major problems with remembering intentions is the lack of retrieval cues, or at least, the lack of *good* retrieval cues. I also mentioned that, to counteract this situation, intention memory seems to be easily triggered by quite marginal cues.

The situation in which remembering has to take place is a critical factor in determining how likely you are to remember. It is therefore useful to distinguish between two broad categories of retrieval situation. These are:

- **event-based tasks**: in which a cue (for example, seeing a shop, or a person, or a book) prompts you to remember your intention, and

- **time-based tasks**: in which you have to remember your intention, without any prompts, at a specific time, or after a specific period has elapsed (for example, checking the oven after half an hour).

As you would expect, event-based remembering is considerably easier than time-based remembering.

In event-based intention memory, we must first notice the cue, then retrieve the intention associated with it. It's easier to notice a cue if it is conspicuous (I'm inclined to say to the males in my household that they wouldn't see something unless it has a flashing neon light)[39] and unfamiliar (we are tuned to pick up new and unexpected things in our

> Actions prompted by events are much easier to remember than actions that you intend to do at a particular time.

environment; the familiar, we just gloss over)[40]. Conspicuousness is of course a function of context, rather than something inherent in the cue itself.

Additionally, if we fix on a category of cues rather than a particular one (say a bookshop, rather than the specific, downtown Borders store), then we're more likely to notice an appropriate example if it is highly typical of its category (we'll notice a "classic" bookshop, but not necessarily one that looks like any other shop, or one that combines selling books with other merchandise)[41].

There is evidence that time-based tasks, although they share common brain regions, activate different areas in the prefrontal cortex than event-based tasks[42].

The anterior prefrontal cortex has been consistently implicated in prospective memory in brain studies, and appears to be of central importance (you'll remember that the prefrontal cortex is crucial for executive function and working memory; *anterior* refers to the section of this region that's closer to the front). However, it is not the only brain region that plays a part in this type of memory. The lateral prefrontal cortex, the parietal cortex (a region to the rear of the head) and precuneus (a region within the parietal cortex), and the anterior and posterior cingulate cortex (areas deeper within the brain, beneath the prefrontal cortex), have all been implicated in prospective memory.

Why am I telling you this? Well, not so that you can memorize the names of the regions! The names aren't important — but what is important is this idea that there is a network across the brain with several disparate regions all doing their bit. This makes it clear that there are several different processes going on, all influenced by different factors.

These two processes — noticing the cue and retrieving the

intention — both activate the same areas, for example, but also show different levels of activation in some of them. Identifying a cue gets the anterior cingulate more excited, while retrieving the intention seems to involve the posterior cingulate and precuneus more.

This is not surprising, if, as is thought, the lateral prefrontal cortex, the anterior cingulate and the lateral parietal cortex make up a control system that maintains visual attention, while the posterior cingulate, precuneus and (again) the lateral parietal cortex are part of the system involved in recalling information (such as what exactly you have to do — the retrospective memory component).

All this makes it clear why you can be good at some parts of the task, but not others — remembering you have to do something but not what it is you have to do, or being perfectly clear on what you have to do but have trouble picking up when to do it.

Why does it matter, on a practical level, why these processes are separate?

Well, partly because different factors affect them, and partly because these two processes operate sequentially (first you notice the cue, then you retrieve the intention) and require you to direct attention in opposite directions. To notice the cue, you must be paying attention to the outside world. To retrieve the intention, you must look within your mind. So, if you're busy holding onto the intention itself (you're driving along thinking, *Got to get the bread*), you risk missing the cue (you go right past the shop), because your attention is in the wrong place.

You have to have faith that your mind will come up with the intention once it sees the cue (which it will if you have linked the two together properly), and concentrate your attention where it should be — on noticing the cue.

Is being too busy a valid excuse?

One of the problems with intention memory is that you usually need to remember the intention while you are engaged in other activities. Remembering to get the bread on the way home. Remembering to take the pie out of the oven when you are watching TV. Remembering to make a dentist's appointment during your working day.

It seems obvious that if you have many demands on your time and, more importantly, on your thoughts, then you will have less working memory available to monitor or review any plans. Certainly, people tend to use being too busy or distracted as an excuse for not remembering. But is it valid? Does being busy really interfere with your recall of intentions?

Although there has been little research to date on this question, it has been shown that remembering is worse when people are required to remember an intention while doing a cognitively demanding task, compared to doing an undemanding task[43]. This is particularly true if the other task involves planning and monitoring (because this interferes with the planning and monitoring requirements of intention memory[44]).

On the other hand, there is some evidence to show that this is true only if the intention is of little personal importance[45].

Moreover, one study suggests that appointments are more easily remembered on more structured days (for example, week days versus weekend days)[46]. Might we make a distinction then, between being busy as part of a well-structured lifestyle, and being busy because you are never quite in control of your life?

> How busy you are may affect how reliably you remember intended activities, but your degree of organization is probably more important.

Circumstances that affect your remembering

Older adults do appear to be more disadvantaged by demanding background tasks[47]. So, although being engaged in other tasks may not be an adequate excuse for younger adults, it is perhaps more reasonable for seniors.

Wanting to remember is not enough!

There is some evidence that the importance of the intention affects whether or not you remember it[48]. Providing a small financial reward for successfully remembering an intention has also been shown to improve memory[49]. However, while personal importance does make it more likely that you will remember an action, it is not as critical as most people imagine. There is no evidence that it plays a *major* part in helping you remember future events.

It is, however, of major importance in determining how badly you feel if you forget! For this reason, perhaps, tasks that involve other people are more likely to be remembered than tasks that are of importance only to you[50]. This may be particularly true for older adults (social importance doesn't seem to affect young adults' prospective remembering[51]).

It is theorized that the importance of an action helps you remember because (put simply), you are more likely to think about it repeatedly.

However, given all the other factors that are of much greater importance in determining whether or not you remember an intention, I hope you can rid yourself of the idea that, if someone forgets your birthday, it means they don't care about you!

Timing and complexity

The importance of timing

One distinction that has been made by researchers[52] is that between:

- **pulses**: actions that can only be carried out during a limited window of opportunity (for example, recording a TV program); and
- **steps**: actions that can be carried out within a longer period of time (for example, making a dentist appointment).

One study[53] found that pulses were remembered better than steps, and also that pulses tended to have greater personal importance and to involve more use of external memory aids. Steps tended to be more flexible. From the details of the study, I would speculate that people may have seen less need to make an effort to remember steps.

However, another study[54] found that, on the contrary, steps were remembered than pulses.

The contradiction in results may well be due to the confounding influences of personal importance and differences in the type of tasks. The steps and pulses in the second study differed only in that the task (making a phone call every day for a specified five day period) needed to be performed either at exactly the same time every day, or between a four hour period (i.e., morning or afternoon). In this circumstance, those required to make the phone call at an exact time forgot more often than those who had more leeway in their timing.

Now this may seem unsurprising, but further analysis of the

results revealed something rather more interesting. The reason why those who had to ring at an exact time were more likely to forget was, quite simply, that they were more likely to use a less effective means of remembering.

Those whose timing had to be exact remembered just as well as those who had a broader window of opportunity, *if they used the same cue*. But those who had to remember exactly were more likely to use an internal/mental cue than an external one (in other words, they simply "relied on their memory"). Comments from some of participants suggest that the task of doing something at the same time every day was seen as relatively easy. They were over-confident.

In this case, then, it was the pulses that people saw as needing less effort.

I would also speculate that there is a perceived difference between an action that needs to be performed, once, at a specific time, and one that you intend to make on repeated occasions at the same time. Please note I said "perceived".

When you plan to do something at the same time every day, you are inclined to see it in terms of a habit, rather than a change in routine. And you are right, if you anticipate that you will find a habit easier to remember. But the benefits of repetition do require the repetition to occur first! There will be no added mnemonic advantage on the first performance of an action, and precious little on the second.

So where does that leave us? Are actions that have to be performed within a narrow time frame easier or harder to remember than those given a broad window of opportunity? I think, in fact, that what these studies indicate is that there is no real difference. The only reason why timing is important is that we alter our strategies, often to the detriment of our performance.

There is one aspect of timing that may affect remembering, however. There is some evidence that remembering intentions is easier in the morning and evening, and worst in the afternoon[55]. This is quite a different pattern to that observed[56] for other types of memory.

> The afternoon is the worst time of day to schedule intended activities.

It has been suggested that the reason may lie in schema we have for times of day — that is, part of our concept of plans involves expectations about different activities 'belonging to' different times of day. It appears that afternoon is the time period with the fewest associated activities, and accordingly, it provides the least support for intended activities. In the same way, it is harder to remember appointments scheduled for the weekend — because there is less structure to the weekend, and thus fewer 'hooks' you can hang an intention on.

The importance of length of time to remember

There is, of course, another aspect of time that is important for prospective memory tasks, and that is the length of time for which you must remember your intention.

On the face of it, it would seem that the longer you must remember your intention, the less likely you are to remember it. Frequency and recency of recollection are, after all, major factors in most remembering, and must, surely, affect the likelihood of your remembering an intention. Interestingly, however, research suggests that the likelihood that you will remember an intention is affected more by whether or not you recall it *at all* during the waiting period than by *how often* you think of it[57].

In other words, reminding yourself of an intention ten times during the interval doesn't substantially improve your chances of remembering at the right time, compared to remembering it once. But remembering it once during that interval makes it appreciably more likely that you'll remember, compared to not remembering it at all during the interval.

Another factor that may be important is the nature and quantity of activities you are engaged in during the period$_{58}$. This is presumably more of a problem over long intervals, and it may also be more of a problem for less important intentions.

Thus, for example, just now I went upstairs to check the mailbox. Passing through the living area, I saw a book I wanted and formed the intention to take it downstairs with me on my way back. I checked the mailbox, came inside, got myself a drink … and went downstairs again without picking up the book. The activities (and particularly, the second one) interfered with my remembering what was, after all, an unimportant intention.

Over a longer interval, even important intentions may be lost. Thus, I go to the library to pick up a book I need. It's a direct journey so there's no problem remembering that intention. But say I decide to combine it with other errands. Perhaps I have a dentist appointment, and decide to do it after that. Perhaps I need to post a parcel as well. The more activities that fill the interval, the greater the chance that one of them will interfere with my remembering of the others. The more "distracting" the activities (a visit to the dentist can be fairly distracting!), the more likely that activity will interfere with your remembering of other intentions.

None of this is a problem if you are aware of the dangers, and the need to form a strategy to assist your memory. For example, if I was afraid I'd forget the library book, and it was important, I'd try to do it first, before the dentist visit. If that wasn't possible, I'd map out my various intentions, mentally itemizing my various errands in the order I intended to accomplish them, and with due awareness of the route I would drive. I might also arrange for some reminder object in a prominent place in the car with me — a library book that needed to be returned, or at a pinch, my library card.

Defining the complexity of an intention memory task

The problem of other activities can usefully be defined in terms of complexity. The following distinctions have been made[59]:

- a **single activity** has a single goal (e.g., remembering to put coffee grounds in the filter jug when making coffee)
- a **dual activity** involves competing goals (e.g., driving home and remembering to buy milk on the way)
- a **simple task** involves monitoring an activity that is to be interrupted (e.g., monitoring your drive home to ensure you notice the store where you are to buy the milk)
- a **compound task** involves monitoring something other than the ongoing task (e.g., any task that occurs at a particular time requires you to monitor the time as well as the ongoing activity).

The distinction between single and dual activity is a somewhat arbitrary one, since any activity usually involves multiple sub-goals (e.g., remembering to put coffee grounds in the filter jug may involve rinsing the filter jug, heating the jug, getting out the coffee grounds, getting a spoon, etc.). The distinction is however a useful one, and in most cases we have no trouble deciding what encompasses a single activity.

The distinction between simple and compound tasks applies only to dual activities; single activities are assumed to be simple.

Let's look at some examples:

- Going to the supermarket to buy several items — this is a single activity, even though multiple items are involved.

- Going to the supermarket after going to the garden center and the library — this is a simple dual activity, because it involves competing goals (your various errands), which are done one after another.

- Going to the supermarket and the library on the occasion of going to pick up a child at the end of school — this is a compound dual activity, because it involves competing goals (your various errands), one of which requires you to monitor the time (a process unrelated to the activity).

Of course, it can be reasonably argued that all intention memory tasks involve monitoring, and more than one activity. At some level, then, all such tasks can be seen as compound dual activities (and perhaps this helps explain the difficulty in remembering intentions!). However, these distinctions can be made at a "commonsense" level, within the context of intention memory tasks, and making these distinctions helps us assess the demands of a specific task.

Thus, by assessing a situation as being both dual and compound, we alert ourselves to the complexity of the situation, and hopefully set in place appropriate strategies to help.

Main points

Activities that have to be done at a particular time are harder to remember than activities that are cued by some event, especially for older people.

Being organized helps you remember future actions and events.

Wanting to remember is not a major factor in determining whether you will.

Intentions that involve other people are more likely to be remembered.

Whether an intention has to be remembered at a specific time or over a broader time frame does not in itself make the intention harder or easier to remember.

The timing of an intention affects remembering indirectly, through your choice of strategy.

Memory for intentions over a short period can be impaired when the intentions are less important and you are engaged in more interesting activities.

Memory for intentions over a long period can be made more difficult by the activities engaged in during that period.

The difficulty of remembering an intention can be measured in part by the specific task's complexity, defined in terms of whether it is single or dual, simple or compound.

Are some people better at remembering intentions?

Earlier, I mentioned that some people may be more prone to absentminded errors than others, but this is largely a function of situational factors rather than fixed ones — lack of sleep, stress, distraction. Some people will be more vulnerable to these factors than others, but there's no particular evidence that age, in and of itself, renders you more absentminded. What about prospective memory?

Age differences

Although people usually worry more about their memory as they get older, this is not necessarily justified. While there are some memory tasks that older adults tend to perform more poorly than younger adults, remembering intentions is not one of them. In fact, some research has found that older adults (in their sixties or seventies) tend to perform better than younger adults at remembering future actions[60].

Two explanations have been suggested for this somewhat surprising finding — neither explanation having anything to do with "natural" ability:

- older adults are more likely to use environmental aids[61];
- older adults tend to lead more routine (structured) lives.

A greater difficulty in remembering time-based activities

One study however, suggests that while older adults may sometimes be better at remembering event-based tasks, they may be poorer than younger adults at remembering time-based tasks[62]. This may reflect the fact that, in daily routine, older adults tend to lead less time-dominated lives. But it also seems that older adults are poorer at monitoring time. This may be related to differences in time perception.

> Older adults tend to find it harder than younger adults to remember time-based tasks.

How do we perceive the passing of time? We are all familiar with its vagaries — how sometimes time passes in a flash, and other times slows to a crawl. Do we measure it by the ticking of a "biological clock"? Or do we judge it on the basis of the events we remember occurring over that time? If so, those who have trouble remembering the intervening events should consistently underestimate the elapsed time. And it does appear that, when given external cues to remind them what has happened over the interval, older adults' estimation of elapsed time lengthens[63].

Some event-based activities may also be harder for older adults to remember

Although in theory older adults are usually at least as good as younger adults at remembering intentions triggered by events, in practice even event-based remembering is affected by age. This is because, in the real world, we usually have to remember our intentions against the background of our daily activities. For a variety of reasons, these daily activities may well be more demanding of cognitive resources for older adults than for younger. This will have an impact on older adults' remembering of intentions.

As we've already discussed, one situation of particular difficulty for older adults is when a remembered intention cannot be performed immediately, but must be held in memory for a brief period. Here is a very familiar scenario. You go to check the mailbox and on the way you recall that you have to ring someone. *I'll do it as soon as I get inside*, you think, but by the time you get back inside, thirty seconds later, you have completely forgotten it.

This sort of forgetting is, indeed, one of those simple memory failures that cause people to think their memory's "going". How can anyone forget so quickly? Something must be wrong.

I hope that the earlier discussion of working memory consoled you with the realization that this sort of forgetting is common, and to be expected, given that unrehearsed information lingers in working memory for less than two seconds.

The trouble is, if the intention "pops up" easily in the first place, we are inclined to believe that it will be held in mind equally easily — that no action is necessary to maintain the thought. While younger adults are equally likely not to consciously rehearse in those circumstances, because of the effect of age on working memory and related capabilities, the failure to rehearse is probably of greater consequence for older adults.

It may also be that older adults are less likely to reformulate their plans. For example, if the intention you have encoded in memory is "Ring Sarah when I get back inside", and you recall this as soon as you get back inside, but decide to put the kettle on first, you need to reformulate your intention as "Ring Sarah when I've put the kettle on". There is some evidence that older adults may encode less precise intentions than younger adults[64].

Main points

Older adults are just as good as younger adults at remembering event-based tasks in optimal circumstances.

Older adults are particularly disadvantaged when they can't act on a remembered intention immediately.

Older adults may find it harder to monitor time accurately.

Individual differences

Clearly some people are better at remembering future events than others. What makes them better at this task? Do they just have a "better memory"? Do they try harder? Are they more practiced? Is it more important to them?

Most of the research into individual differences in planning memory has been concerned with age differences, but there are some indications of other personality differences that might influence your ability to remember the future.

Genes

Because genes are often regarded as an excuse, I want to start by emphasizing that genes are not destiny. Genes are predisposition; whether that predisposition develops into behavior is not the work of the gene alone.

For example, a particular gene variant is associated with a greater risk of depression — but only for those whose childhood home environment was emotionally cold and unsupportive. There is a gene variant that is linked to Alzheimer's disease, but that doesn't mean you are doomed to develop Alzheimer's. It does mean that if you have this variant, you should take steps to take all the actions that research has found will prevent or delay Alzheimer's — actions which are often of much greater benefit to people with this gene variant.

So, with this very firm caveat in mind, I note that research suggests that genes can affect prospective memory. Specifically, a study found that healthy, dementia-free older adults (average age 77 years) who had the 'Alzheimer's gene' (the e4 allele of the apolipoprotein E gene) did significantly worse on a prospective memory task than their counterparts who didn't have the gene variant[65]. This gene variant is found in around 15% of the population.

Another gene that may affect prospective memory was identified in a twin study involving some 2000 female twins aged between 19 and 85 (average age 51 years). The study found a reasonably high degree of inheritability for prospective memory, and a likely candidate gene. This gene (known as the SCAD gene) is expressed in the brain, and in the hippocampus in particular, in the generation of theta waves. Evidence suggests these waves, which are associated with learning and memory, may particularly reflect central executive function[66, 67].

Interestingly, and confirming the belief that prospective and retrospective memory abilities have little correlation, the study found a completely different chromosome implicated for retrospective memory (chromosome 18 rather than chromosome 12).

Personality differences

Some people are plagued by involuntary thoughts repeatedly reminding them of things they have to do. Other people only think about their intentions when they don't expect to be reminded by some environmental cue. You would think there would be a difference between these two groups of people in how likely they are to remember their intended tasks, but in fact, no difference has been found$_{68}$. (This is consistent with the finding that remembering many times is not necessarily more helpful than remembering once).

Some people are, however, better than others at remembering intentions. These people tend to be well-organized. This is not surprising. The effective use of environmental aids depends on developing appropriate routines, on having specific places for reminder cues, on using them as a matter of routine. Mental strategies too, are assisted by mental organization. Memories are found by following the links between memories. Encoding your memories for easy recall requires organization.

> Well-organized people tend to be better at remembering future actions and events.

There is also some evidence that people with the so-called Type A personality (associated with a strong sense of time urgency, an intense need to complete tasks, and a preoccupation with meeting deadlines) are more likely to remember intentions than those with the opposing Type B personality — but only when the task either involves other people or is of personal importance[69].

Anxiety and depression

There are two principal emotions that are thought to affect prospective remembering: depression and anxiety. Although research has not found consistent effects, there does seem to be enough evidence to suggest that, yes, both depression and anxiety can affect this type of remembering —*but* exactly how depends on circumstance.

The effects of emotion on prospective remembering are thought to be related to executive function — in this case, through the redirection of attentional resources.

It's theorized[70] that depression reduces the ability to perform tasks requiring working memory, because some of your working memory capacity is taken up with irrelevant thoughts (such as things that are bothering you). This effect will be greatest when the tasks require a lot of attentional control, such as remembering to do something at 2 o'clock. This effect, however, is not expected to occur if remembering the intention is very important to the person.

This theory makes a lot of sense, and predicts that whether depression will have a noticeable effect on your remembering will depend on how many other things are calling for your attention, and how much attention the remembering needs — for example, it should be more noticeable for a time-based task than an event-based one (which is what studies show).

The story is a little more complicated for anxiety. This is because anxiety seems to have two opposing effects: it increases motivation, and, like depression, it uses up valuable attentional resources[71]. The result of this interplay is that anxiety may in some circumstances improve prospective remembering (because of the increased motivation), and in other circumstances impair it (because of the decreased attention).

More specifically, anxious people will probably do better at remembering intentions when the task is easy or very important — because their anxiety will make them give priority to the remembering task. But if they think the task is too hard for them, or isn't very important, the reduced attentional resources will mean that they're more likely to forget.

Again, there is some evidence to support this theory.

Other disorders

Studies suggest more prospective memory problems among smokers (with problems increasing with greater nicotine use), regular Ecstasy users, and heavy drinkers[72].

Greater prospective memory problems have also been found in people with mild Parkinson's disease, schizophrenia, stroke, head injury, and children with ADHD[73].

In all these cases, the culprit again seems to be executive dysfunction.

Back to working memory and attentional control

So what does all this suggest? It seems clear that various biological and emotional factors can impact your prospective memory. Your genes may predispose you to weakness in prospective memory, unrelated to your retrospective memory.

Personality factors, emotional state, drug and alcohol use, can all affect your prospective memory. But none of these should be taken as an excuse for failing to remember future plans and events. Rather, they should provide motivation to find and use effective strategies — a far more important factor in determining your success.

They also all point in the same direction: problems in working memory and attention.

Evidence suggests that, when the task is complex (and most prospective memory tasks in the real world are complex), executive functioning — your working memory capacity — is a very important component$_{74}$.

It's been suggested, in fact, that the principal reason why we fail to remember to do something at the right time or on the right occasion comes down to a restriction of attentional capacity, for one reason or another. It may be because your capacity is impaired due to age or ill health or brain damage; it may be because it is temporarily restricted because it's too busy with other things$_{75}$.

Even when we think we have completely forgotten an intention and our remembering seems perfectly spontaneous, it doesn't mean that our attention wasn't engaged at some level. Our feelings are an unreliable guide. Noticing something that reminds you of an intention does require your executive control system to have, tucked away somewhere, a little note. Which means that some part of your working memory is taken up with this, even if only a small part.

Just how much of your working memory capacity will be taken up with this depends on many of the factors we've discussed, such as how complex the task is, how important it is to you, and also how difficult it is to spot the cue$_{76}$.

That's why, when you're assessing how demanding a task is, you should be thinking in terms of attentional demands.

> **Main points**
>
> Getting older is no excuse for forgetting future plans.
>
> Age differences are more pronounced for time-based tasks than event-based tasks.
>
> Remembering whether you have performed some action is more difficult when the action is a habitual one.
>
> Being organized helps you remember future actions and events.
>
> Conditions (temporary or state) that reduce your working memory capacity make remembering an intention a more demanding task.

Review

Remembering your intentions is made difficult by the lack of natural triggers. However, intentions are more easily triggered than other memories. Intentions can be recalled in response to quite marginal cues.

Remembering intentions is also complicated by time factors:

- remembering an intention requires you not only to remember the intention, but also to remember it *at an appropriate time*
- intentions often must be remembered for a lengthy period of time
- intentions may sometimes need to be carried out within a very narrow time-frame.

Intentions that you need to do at a particular time are much harder to remember than intentions that wait upon events.

A time-based task may be made easier to remember by transforming it into an event-based task.

The many different intentions we hold in memory form a hierarchy based on their time-frame, their importance, and their complexity. We use prioritizing strategies to order these goals, but changing circumstances sometimes affects our planned order.

When circumstances change, intentions are more likely to be forgotten.

When an intention is postponed, you may need to reformulate your intention, specifying the new situation in which you will accomplish the intention.

General strategies for remembering intentions

Hopefully you now have a good understanding of the principles involved in remembering intentions. Now we'll apply them.

Let's look first at the common strategies people use.

Strategies people use

Here are the three most commonly used strategies for remembering to do things[77]:

- writing yourself reminder notes
- asking someone to remind you
- repeating your intention to yourself over and over again (mental rehearsal)

All of these can be effective strategies. Writing yourself reminders and rehearsing the information are more likely to be effective than asking others to remind you, however.

General strategies

Remind me, will you?

Despite the popularity of this strategy, it is not particularly effective. It's popular because it's easy, not because it works.

It *can* work, of course. How effective it is depends in part, of course, on the reliability of the person you ask. But it also depends on how and when they remind you.

> Effectiveness depends on:
> - the *reliability* of the person reminding you
> - the *accessibility* of the person reminding you
> - *how* the reminder is phrased
> - your willingness to be reminded (your willingness to be dependent on another)

Reliance on another predisposes you not to bother trying to remember yourself, thus making forgetfulness much more likely when the person is not available to remind you[78].

Although, in general, relying on others to remind you is not recommended as a particularly reliable strategy, remembering to take medication may be a specific task that can benefit from such a strategy.

Relying on another to remind you is best when the other person is reliable, in close contact with you, and has a vested interest in you remembering.

More medication errors are made by elderly people living alone[79], and many people cite their spouse's reminders as a factor in helping them take medication at the right time[80]. Spousal support has also been found to be a significant factor in medication adherence in men who have had coronary episodes[81].

> **Main points**
>
> Writing yourself reminders is the most common strategy for remembering intentions.
>
> Asking someone else to remind you is also a popular strategy, but not particularly effective.
>
> Asking a spouse or partner to remind you may be effective when the intended action is one in which they have a vested interest.

Effective strategies for remembering intentions

Effective strategies for remembering future actions and events may be divided into two types:

- *mental* strategies that involve thinking about your intentions in such a way as to enhance remembering, and
- *environmental* strategies that involve using objects in your environment as retrieval cues.

Mental strategies for better recall

Link the intention with its circumstance

There are two parts to remembering an intention:

- the intention itself

- the circumstances in which the intention is to be achieved (the **target situation**).

For example, if you need to take a pill after lunch, *taking the pill* is the intention, and *after lunch* is the target situation.

Effectively remembering intentions involves linking the target situation with the intended activity. Remember, memory needs to be triggered by something. In the case of an intention, you want the target situation to automatically trigger the associated memory for the intended activity (in this example, finishing lunch needs to trigger your remembrance that you have to take your pill).

> When you encode your intention, and whenever you remind yourself of it, always think of the circumstances in which you will carry out the task as well.

To improve your memory for future actions, you need to strengthen the link between the target situation and the task. Links are strengthened by repeated use. Thinking of both (situation and activity) at the same time will strengthen the link between them.

Important variations in the target situation

It is the target situation rather than the intention that is of primary importance in determining your strategy. Target situations may be classified as:

- event-dependent
- time-dependent
- opportunistic.

Let's look at each of these in turn.

Event tags

Often a particular intention is linked to a specific event. For example, I must buy some stamps when I go to the supermarket this evening. I must remember to ask Sophie about cat vaccinations when I see her at the party on Saturday.

There are several characteristics of target situations that can affect our memory for the future task. Probably the most important is how common the event is. Is it an unusual event? Is it something that occurs every day? Is it something you would notice?

Going to the supermarket is clearly not an uncommon event, and is thus not a particularly effective reminder in itself.

Going to a party, particularly a specific party (*Paul's 40th birthday party at the Skyline restaurant*), is a much more remarkable event and will be a better cue.

> The more unusual (noticeable) the event, the better a reminder it will be.

Time tags

Remembering activities that must be carried out at a particular time is in general more challenging than remembering tasks that are responses to events. Time-tagged tasks require you to monitor the passing of time in addition to the normal requirements of event-tagged tasks.

Some intentions must be performed within a narrow time frame (*by 6 o'clock*), while others have looser requirements (*before the new year*). Some intentions must be remembered over a long time period (weeks, months). These are factors that must be taken into account when choosing your strategy.

General strategies

And, of course, time in itself is not particularly memorable. After all, 6 pm occurs every day. Unless something in particular happens at 6 pm (such as dinner or a TV program), we are unlikely to notice its arrival without some sort of environmental reminder (or nagging yourself to note the time). Dates, too, roll on day after day in a predictable manner. It is events (someone's birthday; the time you have morning tea; the day and time of your favorite TV program) that render a time or day or date noticeable.

> Time tags need events to make them noticeable.

In the absence of a naturally occurring event, you need to provide one — a timer, an alarm, some sort of environmental aid — that calls your attention to the specified time or date.

Opportunistic planning

Intentions that aren't tagged to a particular time or event, but simply wait upon an appropriate opportunity, are even more problematic. For example, the vague thought, "I must get some more stamps", if left as a vague intention, will probably only be triggered if you are actually presented with some undeniable cue (seeing stamps for sale) at an appropriate time.

Opportunistic intentions tend to be the worst remembered. It is therefore the type of intention that requires the most strategic thinking.

> Intentions that are not tagged to a specific time or event are the most difficult to remember.

Recognizing opportunities

The main problem with opportunistic planning is the need to recognize appropriate situations. If you think about those circumstances that will be appropriate at the time you form the intention, you stand a much better chance of remembering to do the task at an appropriate time.

Much of the problem comes from a too-specific definition of the appropriate circumstances. In our earlier example, *get stationery* was forgotten because it was linked to *post office* rather than the broader circumstance *place that sells stationery*.

> You'll remember opportunistic intentions better if you encode them with appropriate opportunities.

When you're considering the information that should be encoded with a particular intention, you should look for features that you're likely to notice. Leaving my son's old shoes at the bottom of the shoe basket won't remind me to get new laces, because I'm not likely to notice them down there. Leaving them out beside the basket will make them much more noticeable — but only for a while. If they stay there for long enough, they'll become an easily ignored, familiar part of the scene.

> You need to encode features of the opportunities that you'll notice.

Choosing distinctive cues

Part of a feature's "noticeability" comes from its distinctiveness — you're not likely to notice details of your everyday environment, things you see every day. But familiarity can also be an advantage. Some things we notice *because* of their familiarity — I notice cars on the road that are the same make as our own; we tend to notice people who remind us of people we know. Other things we notice because they have a particular interest for us. Wherever I go, even if I'm just driving past, I always notice bookshops. My father, a keen fisherman, trained me to always look at rivers as I go over or past them. Although I myself have no particular interest in the state of the river, I still look automatically.

But becoming a good rememberer of future actions is also about training yourself to recognize the less obvious opportunities. Recognizing such opportunities involves a certain amount of thought. Such thinking is more effective if done at the time you form the intention (when it will become part of the memory code for that intention), than at a later time.

> Train yourself to notice less obvious opportunities. Encode these with the intention.

Thus, with our stationery example, instead of thinking *post office* or *place that sells stationery*, you could have spent a little time thinking of all the various places available to you where you could buy the stationery you want.

When predictive encoding is the best strategy

Predictive encoding is the name for this strategy of encoding the various situations, both obvious and obscure, in which you can carry out your intention[82].

The predictive encoding strategy will be more effective in some circumstances than others. For example, when the connection between cue and intention is glaringly obvious, the deliberate encoding of anticipated cues with the intention is of course less necessary.

Predictive encoding provides the biggest advantage when:

- cues are hard to match to intentions
- your time and concentration are limited at the time of carrying out the intention
- your intention is one you infrequently experience

- some of the opportunities to achieve the intention aren't obvious.

Research also suggests that there is some advantage in working out how to carry out your intentions yourself. But being told how by someone else is still better than not having a plan at all.

> Predictive encoding is most useful when opportunities are rare, obscure, unfamiliar, or likely to occur when your attention is limited.

Working out your plan

Just how specific should your planning be?

Let's go back to our example of buying stationery. Now this stationery could be widely available in places that only sell a small range of stationery, or it might require a specialist shop. If it's widely available (implying many potential opportunities), then you will clearly want to encode quite an abstract plan —*place that sells stationery* is going to be much more successful than thinking only of one specific place. However, if it can only be bought in one particular place, you need to link that specific place to your intention. You can broaden it in other ways however.

For example, there are stationery requirements that I can reliably fill in only one shop. That shop is on a particular route for me, but it's not a route I use very often. Therefore, when I need to buy stationery, I not only link it with that shop, I also link it with the other shops in the vicinity that I sometimes visit. So if I decide to go to any of those shops, it will trigger a reminder that while I'm there, I also need to visit the stationery shop.

As a general rule, more abstract plans are better than very specific ones. Abstract plans open you to noticing more opportunities. If you encode only very specific opportunities, you are much less likely to notice other unanticipated opportunities that would allow you to achieve your goal.

Think about broad types of opportunities rather than specific ones.

On the other hand, you *are* more likely to recognize that specific event or item as an opportunity to achieve your intention. For this reason, even when encoding an abstract plan (*place that sells stationery*), it is worth thinking of as many specific examples as possible, to prime you to notice opportunities as they arise.

Remember too, that the most effective type of reminder is one that refers both to the task *and* the circumstances in which the task is to be carried out. Being reminded of the circumstances alone (e.g., *Remember Lucy's coming!*) doesn't help at all. Being reminded of the task alone *may* help (e.g., *Remember to give Lucy the book!*) — but perhaps only when the task automatically calls forth the circumstances in which it is to be carried out. The best reminder has both: *Remember to give Lucy the book when she comes!*[83]

Reminders to yourself and others should include both intention and situation.

Interestingly, given the emphasis most popular memory programs place on imagery, it has been found that when people are told to imagine themselves in the situation performing the task, this has no additional benefit over the simple reminder of the task and the situation. That is, both help to improve memory, but the verbal reminder is at least as good as the reminder involving imagery (and in fact, in the laboratory situation, was better[84]).

Verbal reminders are at least as good as visualizing.

Planning style

There are four basic planning styles:

- List/time-based
- List/event-based
- Chart/time-based
- Chart/event-based

Let's see what examples of those might look like for a complex medication task.

List/time-based

8am	blood pressure tablets
8.30	diabetes tablets
12.30	diabetes tablets
6pm	diabetes tablets
10pm	allergy tablets

List/event-based

get up	blood pressure tablets
with breakfast:	diabetes tablets
with lunch:	diabetes tablets
with dinner:	diabetes tablets
go to bed:	allergy tablets

Chart/time-based

	Mon	Tue	Wed	Thu	Fri	Sat	Sun
7							
8	bp	bp	bp	bp	bp	bp	bp
9	d	d	d	d	d	d	d
10							
11							
12							
1	d	d	d & c	d	d	d	d
2							
3							
4							
5							
6	d	d	d	d	d	d	d
7							
8							
9							
10	a	a	a	a	a	a	a

Chart/event-based

	Mon	Tue	Wed	Thu	Fri	Sat	Sun
get up	bp	bp	bp	bp	bp	bp	bp
breakfast	d	d	d	d	d	d	d
lunch	d	d	d & c	d	d	d	d
dinner	d	d	d	d	d	d	d
go to bed	a	a	a	a	a	a	a

A comparison of the success of each of these types reveals, unsurprisingly, that plans that reduce the attentional requirements of the task are the most effective.

Thus, as we already know, an event-based plan is generally preferable to a time-based one (because less monitoring is needed), and similarly, a chart is generally preferable to a list, because it is easier to read and understand.

However, some tasks will lend themselves better to a list, so you do need to be sensitive to the requirements of the task.

Understandably, items that don't need to be remembered every day are more likely to be forgotten, and it is for events like these that a written implementation plan is most useful.

Plans such as these have been found to be particularly valuable for people with psychological problems, such as schizophrenia, frontal lobe damage, and heroin addiction. Although not investigated, it seems likely that implementation plans might also be particularly useful for anyone with attentional and executive function problems.

Main points

If your intention involves specific items, or a specific place, explicitly link these to your intention.

If your intention can be achieved using any of a number of items, or in various situations, give thought to the *type* of items or situations.

Train yourself to notice opportunities to achieve your goals:

- practice **plan generation** (thinking about novel ways of achieving your goals); and
- **situational awareness** (learning what to notice).

Plans you make yourself work better than plans other peoplehave told you, but both help you remember your intentions.

Actions that must be carried out at specific times may be hindered by the attention diverted to checking the time. Arrange for some environmental trigger to remind you of the time.

Using environmental memory aids

In many circumstances environmental strategies are better than mental strategies for remembering future actions or events.

Environmental memory aids include such strategies as writing yourself reminders, tying a knot in your handkerchief, setting an alarm on your watch, etc. (I talk a little about high-technology memory aids in Appendix B).

Environmental memory aids are the most frequent strategy people use to help them remember future actions and intentions. There is good reason for this.

> Environmental aids provide cues for future remembering.

Why environmental memory aids are a useful strategy

Remember, one of the problems with intention memory is that you can't rely on retrieval cues spontaneously appearing. While memory about the past is recalled to mind by the appearance of cues, memory for the future often requires you to remember without any prompts.

The solution is obvious: provide yourself with retrieval cues.

Put like that, it is clear that the contempt some people show for the use of environmental aids is unwarranted. Memory *requires* something to trigger it. Providing yourself with a trigger is simply commonsense.

Learning to use environmental memory aids

But using aids such as Post-it notes, shopping lists, calendars, diaries, alarms, and so on, is not as simple a strategy as it may appear. It is not merely a matter of telling yourself, for example: *Well, from now on, I'm going to start remembering to write things down.* The effective use of environmental aids requires you to develop appropriate habits.

> To use environmental aids effectively you must use them habitually.

Habit is the key to success. If you don't use a calendar as a matter of habit, it's no good to you. If you don't have a specific place for reminder notes, you'll probably often miss seeing them in time. If you're not used to listening for a timer, you probably won't even notice it (how else can we explain the fact that I can hear the oven timer go off when I'm at the other end of the house, whereas my partner can't hear it even when he's in the same room?).

Building habits is a matter of reminding yourself to keep doing something until you no longer need the reminder. Building habits is simply a matter of repeating an action often enough. But some habits are easier to learn than others.

What makes a habit easy to acquire?

The best way to learn a new habit is to make sure your environment is set up to facilitate those habits. Take into consideration your present habits and routines. Work to fit your new routine into your existing pattern of behavior.

> Forming new habits is easier if they fit into your existing routine.

In the next chapter, we'll look at specific examples of how to do that.

We have been keeping an engagement diary for the last 19 years. Every day, we consult the diary and often make a list of things that we should do that day or things that should happen, e.g. people calling etc. We leave the list in a prominent place - it saves having to go to the diary to keep checking. Graham says he gets a great deal of satisfaction from crossing off the items on the list as he performs the tasks.

Win, retired school teacher, 82

We have a whiteboard at home and everyone writes their activities or wants on it (kids have learned they are more likely to get what they want this way). Kids have to write times for sport on the whiteboard.

Judy, researcher

I keep lists on my computer so they can be updated easily, e.g. lists of what to pack for tramping, for family camping trips, or for international travel. One of those lists is important dates. At the end of each month I check my dates list, and copy anything important for the coming month into my diary. The diary is a big A4 hardback and everything gets copied into it: work, family dates, appointments, everything. My diary is always with me if I'm at home or at work, usually open on my desk. If I ever lose my diary, I'm doomed.

Anthony, lecturer, 45

Strategies for specific tasks

We've looked at how planning memory works, and those principles that help us determine the broad strategies that will be effective in helping us remember intentions better. We've looked at these broad strategies. But the key to improving your memory is understanding

- how memory domains process information in different ways, and
- that effective memory strategies tend to be very specific.

To truly improve your memory habits, you must practice these situation-specific strategies.

Let's look at some common memory situations:

- Remembering appointments
- Remembering birthdays and anniversaries
- Remembering indeterminate arrangements
- Remembering errands/tasks
- Remembering to take medicine

Remembering appointments

Using environmental aids

We are all familiar with the various environmental aids for remembering appointments. The most common are of course calendars and diaries. Making notes on a calendar is a very effective strategy — a study into the use of memory strategies found it was rated as the easiest to use (out of twenty environmental and mental memory strategies) and had the second highest dependability rating[85].

But of course, the effectiveness of this strategy depends on your habits. How good are you at remembering to write notes on the calendar? How often do you check it to see what's written there?

As I have said, using environmental aids effectively requires you to set up your environment to facilitate useful habits.

For example, I made a major lifestyle improvement many years ago when I set up a "control center" in my home. Above the phone in our main living area, we put a whiteboard (for writing information, like messages and lists), a cork board (for lists of phone numbers, "telephone trees", business cards for tradespeople, ads torn from the newspaper, etc.), and a calendar which shows a month at a time with large boxes for each day.

Being located near the phone helps with writing things down because a lot of arrangements are made via the phone. It also means that you visit the place regularly.

Now a few problems *have* developed over time with this strategy. When we purchased a cordless phone, it meant that (a) we were less likely to be at that particular phone when we made an arrangement, and (b) we visit the control center less often.

However, the phone books are also kept there, and that particular phone incorporates the answerphone for our household, thus still ensuring it gets visited during the day. Moreover, it is right in the middle of our living area, so we can't really avoid it. And equally important, we had already developed the habit of using the control center.

An addendum to the strategy involves the fact that I spend a good part of the day in my office downstairs. Where, of course, I have a phone. But there's no point having two control centers, and although I'm in my office every day, it is still not the *household* nerve center, and it is household arrangements we are talking of here. Thus, if I happen to be in the office when I make or confirm an arrangement, I immediately make a note and leave it on a corner of my desk (items that need to be taken upstairs are always put in that same place).

Most homes probably have around three or four areas where household members spend most of their time. Multiplying control centers is not however a good idea. While you might have subsidiary arrangements for subordinate locations, you need to have a single place where all household arrangements are recorded. This needs to be:

- highly visible
- located in a main traffic area
- close to the main telephone.

Having set up your control center, you need to get into the habit of using it. Initially this may be difficult. Its difficulty will be directly related to how well you have arranged your environment. The more you have taken into consideration your existing habits, the more easily this new habit will be to acquire. Remember, there are two parts to this strategy: remembering to record the information, and remembering to check the record.

Both aspects must be taken into consideration.

Thus, for example, you might decide that the only way to make sure you see the calendar is to hang it right beside the front door. But if this position doesn't also facilitate you recording the information, it won't work.

> [my] appointment diary is invaluable and comes with me wherever I go, though mainly to check times.
>
> Alma, retired nurse, 82

Using a mental strategy

How can we use our knowledge of how intention memory works to improve our memory for appointments?

Appointments are clearly time-based events. But time is not simply one thing — if we have an appointment at 2 pm on the 15th of May, we don't necessarily (or even usually) remember it as: "2 pm, May 15". If you make the appointment in a preceding month, you will probably initially simply encode it as "in May", or "next month". When you hit May, you might recode it as "middle of the month". As the date creeps closer, it might become "next Tuesday". Depending on your other commitments, that may include the time, "2 pm next Tuesday", or less specifically, "next Tuesday afternoon". Or it may be that the time of day doesn't concern you until the day itself.

The point is, the time tag of a future event changes, becoming more specific, as the gap between your present moment and the future event closes. Of course all the information is there in your head, in your memory code, right from the beginning — but the code changes in subtle ways reflecting different emphases.

For example, here is our possible memory code for a dentist appointment again:

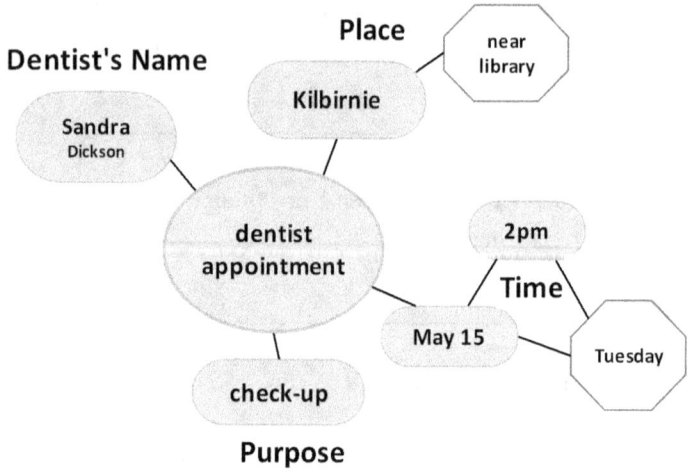

A memory code is a network of linked information, but all pieces of information aren't equal. Some are given more weight. For example:

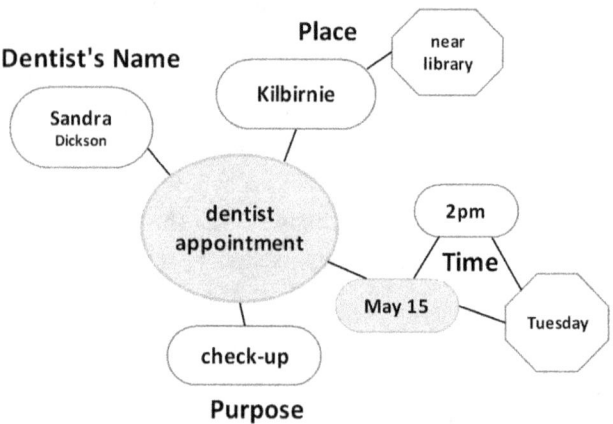

And this weighting can change:

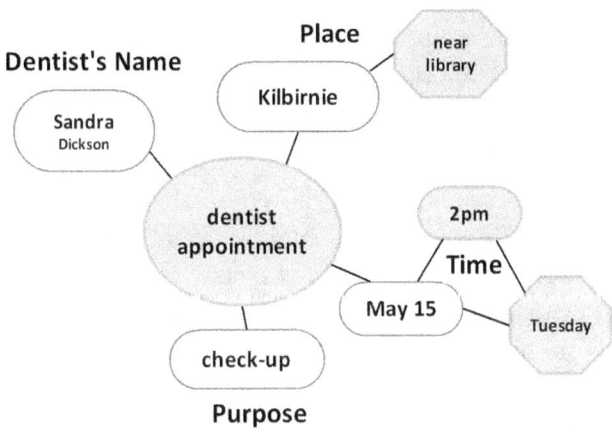

As the date grows closer, the date itself becomes less important, and the day becomes the point you focus on. Thus, as the date gets closer, your time tag might change from *next month* to *mid-May* to *next Tuesday* to *tomorrow*. If you don't think of it in those intervening weeks, your memory won't have the chance to re-code, and you are much less likely to recall it without external prompting.

This is why it's best if you can link the time tag to an event.

If you can't link it to an event, you could use a mnemonic to remember the specific date. The coding mnemonic is useful for remembering numbers, and thus dates and times (see Appendix C).

Relying on others

Dentists' appointments are a prime example of a situation when using others to help you remember can be an effective strategy. One study found that reminders by mail resulted in 84% of appointments kept, compared to 80% when the reminder was by telephone, and only 55% (!) when no reminder was made[86]. The longer the interval between making the appointment and keeping it, the more effective reminders are. Another study found reminders almost doubled the number of people keeping their appointments when the appointments were made more than 15 days earlier[87].

Many professionals now offer this service. I imagine it is particularly useful when the patient is reluctant to keep the appointment (which is presumably why this service is offered more by dentists than any other professionals), since memory failure is not the only reason people fail to keep appointments. Having your dentist or doctor remind you when your appointment is imminent is a good idea when you fear a failure of nerve as much as a failure of memory!

Remembering anniversaries and birthdays

There are two aspects to the common problem of remembering personally important dates. The first is simply the problem of remembering the date *at all*— knowing that your friend's birthday is on the 24th of May, rather than *sometime in May*, *late May*, or *around the 23rd/24th*. The second problem is remembering it at the appropriate time (in time to do something about it, or simply on the day itself, to remember to wish them a Happy Birthday).

The first problem is not in fact the province of planning memory. It is a fact, and belongs in a quite separate memory domain. Nevertheless, it is a prerequisite of your remembering the fact *at the appropriate time*, and so I'll touch on it briefly.

Using environmental aids

The simplest way of ensuring your grasp of the essential fact is to write it down! Granted, this is obvious, but it's surprising how often it isn't done. Indeed, I must confess that I myself was confused about a family member's birthday date for decades, without actually going to the (minimal) effort of writing it down.

There are two main reasons for this. As always, the most important is the failure to see the need. Every year I would think, *Is it the 5th or the 6th?* Every time I found out which it was, I would think, *oh yes, of course*. And believed that *this time*, I'd remember it.

I should have known better. I did know better. The memory I was reinforcing was the memory of that confusion, not the memory of the correct fact.

The second main reason for failing to record the information is that you have no specific place to record it.

I used to have no place where I recorded birthdays because I had no trouble remembering the birthdays of (almost all) those close to me. But this was largely a function of a small family, and a great deal of luck in the placing of those birthdays next to or on **landmarks** (of which more presently). But inevitably the numbers of friends and family whose birthdays should be remembered has increased, and inevitably, more and more of these dates have no particular memorial quality, and a physical record has become a necessity.

Diaries frequently have a place in them for recording birthdays, but this is an unsatisfactory place to record information that you need year after year. Who wants to re-write the list every year? Using your address book for this purpose is a better idea.

There are two ways you can record birth dates in an address

book. Which way is preferable depends on how you're going to use it. If you usually remember birthdays in the appropriate month (*Oh, it's May — now I know there's someone's birthday I have to remember*), then a list of birthdays is the best idea. If your problem is usually an uncertainty about a particular person's birthday (*Isn't Peter's birthday sometime soon?*), then noting birth dates under the person's name is probably a better strategy.

This is particularly useful when you're at the time of life when all your friends are having children (or grandchildren). A note under the names of your friends and relations of the names and

> On the wall of our toilet is a birthday calendar (also includes some anniversaries). We have most of our family, relations and friends on this and also have included their birth years so we can work out how old they are!
>
> This works really well – most days there is someone that we remember or contact for their birthday and most of our friends will say 'you must have been to the toilet today!' when we say Happy Birthday to them ...
>
> Jeanette, 64
>
>
> I have a small notebook for birthdays, anniversaries and whoever I owe a letter. One page for each month.
>
> Lenie, 76
>
>
> Birthday book and also calendar in obvious place for birthdays. I always copy the birthdays for the month on to my kitchen calendar and into my diary.
>
> Mollie, pharmacist, 73

birth dates of their children / grandchildren is a good way to keep track of an ever burgeoning problem.

Some people have so many friends and family to keep track of that they have a special "Birthday Book". If you're in this position, a better idea is the "Birthday Calendar". This calendar has no days, only dates, and is therefore able to be used year after year. It thus serves both purposes — as a permanent record of the dates to be remembered, and a reminder at the appropriate time.

Using a mental strategy

Landmarks are features of the environment that help you remember location — where you are, where something is. We navigate by landmarks (*Turn right at the service station, go three blocks, then turn left at the lights, you'll see a bright pink house, and we're just two houses down on the opposite side*).

A landmark can also be a more abstract concept. When talking about our memory for past events, "landmarks" refer to those events that we use to date our unrolling memory. *Oh, that happened the summer I went sailing in the Sounds. That was around the time I started in the bookshop. That was before I was married.* And so on.

As I said, we don't tend to remember dates and times without reason. What we remember are events.

> Link dates to landmark dates for better remembering.

The reason I have always had so little trouble remembering my family's birthdays is that I have been extraordinarily lucky with landmarks. My mother's birthday is exactly one month after mine — same day, one month later. My sister's birthday is on a public holiday. My partner's birthday is the day before my mother's. His sister's is the day before *my* sister's (Is this spooky or what?). My children ... I have no trouble remembering my children's birthdays. But I have to admit, this is not because of the deep emotion of their births. The experience of giving birth means I won't forget the day (and preceding night) — but the actual dates? Why should I remember the dates? Why should emotion score the date in my brain?

I remember my children's birthdays because over the course of their existence, I have been required to remember it so often. All those times I've filled out forms with their birth dates on. All those parties I've had to plan.

If you don't have a landmark, repetition will do it.

But landmarks are incredibly useful, and if there isn't a naturally occurring one, you can attempt to create one. If the connection is a little strained, you can use repetition to strengthen it. Thus, if my partner's birthday had been five days before my mother's, I could have made sure that connection was firmly in mind, by repeating it a few times (preferably at increasingly spaced intervals — say, a couple of times when I first thought of it, again a few hours later, then the next day, then a few days later).

You might say, *well, if I have to rehearse the thing anyway, why not just rehearse the date itself?* But the connection to a landmark is naturally stronger than the date itself, and thus it requires less effort to get it fixed in memory, and the memory is likely to be more durable.

> I usually tie in the year with something in my life which happened near to the same time. The month in most cases is with me. The date sometimes needs to be looked up.
>
> Alma, retired nurse, 82

Remembering arrangements

Arrangements are less specific than appointments. You might promise to have something done "by next month". You might arrange with a friend that you will have lunch "sometime next week". You might promise your child that you will arrange for their friend to come and play "soon".

Because there is no link to a time or place, such arrangements tend to be more easily forgotten without reminders from the other people concerned. But apart from the fact that few of us like to be nagged, it's not particularly pleasant to acquire a reputation as someone who won't remember without being reminded. Clients and colleagues are likely to believe your unreliability extends to other aspects of your work; friends are likely to believe your forgetfulness is an indication of indifference; children even more so.

What can we do to improve our memory for these promises?

We have to provide what's lacking. A time or event tag.

Using environmental aids

A calendar can still be a useful aid, even though the arrangement has no specific date.

Instead of recording the arrangement for the day on which it will occur (which in this case has yet to be determined), you simply make up a deadline. If it's a social arrangement, make a decision as to when you should have made a specific arrangement by. Make a note on your calendar (I usually add an exclamation mark for these types of reminders, to indicate that they are "to do" instructions). If it's work-related (in the broadest sense of the word — whether it's voluntary work for an organization you belong to, or work for a client or employer), then you probably need several reminders:

Mon	Tues	Wed	Thurs	Fri	Sat	Sun
12 Report due in 3 wks!	13	14	15	16	17	18
19 Report due in 2 wks!	20	21	22	23	24	25
26 Finish report this wk!	27	28	29	30 Report due!!	31	

Better yet is if you break down the task into a series of sub-tasks, making your reminders more specific:

Mon	Tues	Wed	Thurs	Fri	Sat	Sun
12 Plan report!	13 Gather info?	14	15 Finish info search!	16 Check out experts!	17	18
19	20	21 Start writing!	22	23 Finish draft!	24	25
26 Finish writing!	27 Finish ref check!	28	29	30 Report due!!	31	

You could of course simply write yourself a reminder note. If the task only involves a single step (such as having to ring your friend and agree on a specific date), then a reminder note is as good as a calendar note — provided that you have a reliable system in place. However, if the task involves a series of time-separated steps, as in the above example, a calendar is clearly preferable.

Using a mental strategy

As I have said, arrangements are more likely to be remembered if tagged to a specific time or event. And events are better than times.

To make it much more likely that you will remember an arrangement therefore, you should, when making the arrangement, link it to a specific event (if only in your head). Thus, you may say to your child, *I'll ring Peter's mother next week,* but in your head you should say, *Ring Sophie after we get back from cricket practice on Tuesday.* Instead of, *I need to have that report done by March 15,* think, *The report needs to be finished before Philip's birthday.*

When making arrangements, link them to a future event.

> Most things that I do are weekly and are at the same time, so when something new pops up I tend to rehearse what I am going to do during the next twenty four hours and I tell the boys, David and anyone else who will listen so that I have a clear picture of it in my head and I tend to remember then
>
> Christine, mother of 4

Remembering errands and chores

The errands we need to do can vary in their requirements, and thus the specific strategy for dealing with them also varies. Sometimes we need to:

- remember to do things at a *specified time* (e.g., on the way home from work; at lunchtime); or
- remember to do things at a *convenient time*; or
- remember to do things *by* a specified date; or
- remember to do things when in a *specified place*; or
- remember to do things when in an *appropriate place*.

As you would expect from our earlier discussion, the critical factor is the degree to which an errand is tied to a time or place.

Using environmental aids

As we have discussed, we can help ourselves remember tasks that are tied to a specified time or date by using reminder notes or calendars. Remembering to do things at a convenient or appropriate time is more problematic.

> If I put letters/checks to pay bills in my pack the night before I inevitably forget to stop at the post office on my way to work - my mind is so busy organizing for the work day ahead I forget about personal stuff - but if I make the effort to take the mail out to the car and put it on the ledge under the clock on the dashboard I notice it when I get in the car as well as when I drive along and - usually - stop outside the post office and do the posting.
>
> Margs, teacher, 49

One way in which environmental aids can help you in that situation is if you use physical objects to remind you.

We all do this occasionally — leaving an empty jar on the kitchen bench to remind us we need more of something; leaving a library book on the table to remind ourselves to return it, etc. But to use this strategy *consistently*, you need to give some thought to incorporating it into your routine. Thus, I have a specific place (one end of a shelf, centrally located) for library books. When they come into the house, I put them there in a pile, and when they're read, they're placed upside-down in another pile. Items that need to be taken out of the house are placed on a horizontal surface right beside the front door. For supermarket items that for some reason I haven't put on the shopping list (perhaps they're unusual items and I want to make sure I get the right brand or type), I place the empty container on the windowsill above the sink.

The point is, you need to establish specific places for classes of items, and you need to get into the habit of looking in those places at the appropriate times. So the places need to be not only specific, but also convenient, appropriate, and consistently used.

Used in this way, physical objects can be very successful prompts. However, when the task is opportunistic — not tied to a specified time or place — using physical objects can be problematic because of the length of time that might occur before you actually decide the opportunity has come. If you see an object repeatedly, it loses its prominence. After a while you don't really see it anymore.

> When visiting on her way home from shopping [my daughter] places food in freezer/fridge at the friend's home and puts her car keys with the food to remember to take it home
> Mollie, pharmacist, 73

Another external aid that many people use for short-term reminders, is writing on the back of the hand. I must admit to being surprised how widespread that habit seems to be — principally, it seems, among people who are not tied to a desk: nurses, builders, tradesmen, teachers.

> I write things on the back of my hand - for instance if the psychologist wants to talk to two boys from my class after lunch and rings to tell me at the beginning of lunch time, I'll write the boys names on the back of my hand so that I'll see the names while I'm reading the class a story after lunch and remember to send them.
>
> I also use this trick for children who keep leaving library books, homework books, poetry books or portfolios at home. Either the child sees it, or the parents do, and the requisite materials appear at school.
>
> Margs, teacher, 49

While physical prompts are useful, the best way to remember opportunistic intentions may be to use a mental strategy.

Using a mental strategy

This situation, of course, calls for the **predictive encoding strategy**. Let's have a look at it in action.

Your intention is to drop off your old spectacles at your optometrist. There's no urgency about this, but you have forgotten to do it the last two times you have been to the optometrist and you're tired of them sitting around gathering dust. It'll be a year or more before you're back at the optometrist, so it's no good tagging it to *going to optometrist*. You need to think of the places you visit in the vicinity of the optometrist, or on the same route. But perhaps this is part of the problem — perhaps it is not on your accustomed routes. So, you think of diversions. What places do you go to that *could* take you past the optometrist? Are there times when you have sufficient time for a brief stop? (It's no good tagging it to an occasion when you're always in a desperate hurry!)

> Tasks are more likely to be remembered if you link them to the circumstances in which they can be achieved.

So, when I despaired of ever remembering the spectacles gathering dust on my windowsill on the occasion of my infrequent checkups at the optometrist, I framed a new intention: *After my son's piano lesson on Thursday (not before because we're always running late), I'll go the other way through Johnsonville, and stop at the optometrist. Put spectacles in my bag when packing the music.*

Here's another example. Say you want to remember to ring a friend with a query, but whenever you think of it, it's never an appropriate time to ring. You need to think about those appropriate times, and link your intention with those circumstances. Thus, *I'll ring Karen on Tuesday after the children are in bed.*

Remembering to take medicine

It is possible to forget that you've taken medicine at a particular time, and take it again, but this kind of memory failure is relatively rare. It is also rare, given a normal memory, to completely forget that you need to take medicine. No, the primary problem with this kind of memory task is that it is time-bound. You have to remember to take the medicine *at a particular time.*

Typically, this is either:

- before meals; or
- after meals; or
- before bed; or
- at a specified number of times during the day.

> Plan to take medicine at landmark events of your day.

The likelihood of your remembering without assistance, and your specific strategy for dealing with it, will vary depending on which of these situations it is.

One common way of dealing with this situation is to leave your medicine in a prominent place. There are two problems with this. Sometimes the medicine needs to be kept in a cool dark place, and often when an object remains in a particular place for a while, the object becomes less noticeable (even if that place is highly visible).

> Place medicine in a location that will be noticeable at the time you take it.

Moreover, while putting your pills in an obvious place will help you remember that you're taking them, it will not necessarily help you remember *at the right time.*

You need to place your medicine where you will notice it at the appropriate time.

If you need to take it before meals, think about what you do just before you start preparing or eating your meal. For example, you could put your pills in the crockery cupboard.

If it's after meals, you could keep them where you eat, or above the kitchen sink.

If it's before bed, you could put them near the bathroom basin, or by your bed, or, if you have a hot drink before retiring, near the kettle.

Medicine that simply needs to be taken a specified number of times during the day, rather than before or after particular events, is somewhat more problematic. On the other hand, it gives you the opportunity to choose times that will be easier for you to remember. Think about your routine. Choose events that facilitate the linking of your new habit to them.

For example, I always find it easier to remember to take medicine after meals, rather than before. This is because I'm usually the one preparing the meal for several people, and I'm too busy to think of anything additional at that time.

Meals are good to use as reminder events because they usually occur several times a day at regular intervals. I say several, to include breaks such as morning and afternoon tea, or late-night suppers. Bed-times — getting out of bed in the morning, and going to bed in the evening — are also good cues. But the critical factor is simply the regularities in your routine. Anything you do every day at around the same time can be used for this purpose.

The other important factor in choosing a cueing event is to think about what you do / where you are for that event, to assess whether there is some appropriate place for your medicine that you will see at the time.

> I only need two tablets a day. I put the bottle next to the teapot in the morning. Make sure to put it away, after I've taken the tablet. The other tablet I take just before I go to bed, so it is part of the going-to-bed routine, making sure doors and windows are shut and locked.
>
> Lenie, 76

What about when you are taking a number of different medications?

When you have several different medications to take, all at different times and frequencies, the burden on memory is of course considerably greater. And of course, for reasons of age and/or health, you are often less cognitively able to deal with this greater burden. In circumstances like this, a schedule is an excellent idea. Post up a chart detailing, hour by hour, what you are to take when (with annotations if they are to be taken before, with, or after meals).

You can also improve your chances of remembering this change in your routine if, when you initially encode the intention, you not only develop a detailed implementation plan (when and where you'll carry out your intention), but spend a few minutes actually visualizing yourself performing the action in those exact circumstances[88]. But don't continue to do that as a reminder, or you'll be confused as to whether you've already done it!

> My husband has a complicated system for ensuring he has his cocktail of medications morning and night, using a Monday-Sunday box for daily and twice daily doses and now a Webster box as well for 3x daily painkillers. When the midafternoon painkiller began not long ago we had great difficulty remembering it, until we set an alarm radio to go on to a station we don't usually listen to in the afternoon. Now if we hear the Hallellujah Chorus bellow out around the house about 3pm we get him another painkiller.
>
> Tish, civil servant, 65

It's also worth noting that early times in the morning appear to be better remembered than evening times[89].

And finally, there's the problem of medication that's taken at longer intervals, say weekly or monthly.

> I need to take medicine — the daily doses are no problem at all — it is simply a daily habit; I need to take one pill weekly — I take it every Wednesday — I rarely forget that one. The one I do forget now and again is a pill I need to take monthly. I have nominated the 29th of each month to take it and I have forgotten that one three or four times over the last 12 months. I usually remember when the next month pops up and I think — Oh Bother!!!
>
> Ann (not her real name), 69

One way to deal with this sort of situation, particularly for a monthly event, is to fill in your calendar with a reminder at the beginning of the year. Another way, particularly for a weekly event, is to tie it to another, more memorable, event. The trick here is to consciously fix the association in your mind between the two events — and not just in a *monthly meeting of garden club —take pill* sort of way, but in a specific *take pill when getting my things ready for the monthly meeting / after the monthly meeting / at lunch before I go to the monthly meeting* way.

Of course, many people are perfectly reliable in taking their medication as part of the normal routine; the problem arises when their routine is disrupted.

> When at the farm I was pressured into cooking for six and was so intent on getting into my old routine, I didn't remember the pills until after lunch — the pills being in my toilet bag, not under my eye. Also happened when on holiday and out of the usual routine.
>
> Betty, retired farmer, 81

Specific strategies

In circumstances like these, you need to have realized ahead of time that the change in your routine will make remembering more difficult, and made a specific plan for dealing with it. To do that, you'll need to know where you'll be and what you'll be doing at the appropriate time.

Summary of memory tasks & appropriate strategies

Memory situation	Environmental aid	Mental strategy
Remembering birthdays and anniversaries	Use a birthday calendar	Link date to landmark date
Remembering appointments	Use calendars/ diaries habitually	Link to a specific time or event
Remembering indeterminate arrangements	Write reminder notes Use physical objects as cues	Link arrangement to a specific time or event
Remembering to take medicine	Place medicine in appropriately visible locations	Link medicine-taking to landmark events of your daily routine

Memory situation	Environmental aid	Mental strategy
Remembering tasks/errands:		
— at a specified time or by a specified date	Use calendars/diaries habitually	Strengthen link between intention and time. Link time to an event if possible
— when in a specified place	Use physical objects as cues	Strengthen link between intended task and place
— at a convenient time	Write reminder notes Use physical objects as cues	Specify convenient occasions, and link these to the task
— when in an appropriate place	Use physical objects as cues	Specify convenient occasions, and link these to the task

Your master strategy

You cannot have a good or bad memory. You will almost certainly have some good memory skills, and some poorer ones. To improve your memory skills in an area in which you are poor, you need to consider the specific memory situations. And you need to practice using appropriate memory strategies in those situations.

You need to be very specific in your planning. You need to think about which specific situations you want to improve, and about the very specific ways in which you can improve them. Because this depends on your personal habits, I cannot provide hard and fast answers for you, but I can help you work out your own.

The first skill you need to practice is assessing the memory task, to help you refine your strategy to make it effective in this particular circumstance.

Assessing memory tasks

There are seven dimensions along which intentions may be assessed:

- **cue**: whether the intention is to be triggered by an *event* or a *time*
- **frequency**: whether the intended action is *habitual* or *infrequent*
- **period**: whether it is to occur in the *short-term* or the *long-term*
- **window**: whether it is to occur in a *narrow* time-frame or a *broader* window
- **person**: whether it is *personal* (involves only you) or *interpersonal* (involves other people)
- **importance**: whether it is *important* or *unimportant*
- **complexity**: whether it is *simple* or *compound*

We can use these dimensions to roughly rate the difficulty of an intention memory task. To do this, we assign 0 to the easier attribute of each pair, and 1 to the more difficult. Thus, an intention scores a 0 for being event-based, and 1 if it is time-based. Here are the values of all the attributes:

	0	1
cue	event-based	time-based
frequency	habitual	infrequent
period	short-term	long-term
window	broad window	narrow window
person	interpersonal	personal
importance	important	unimportant
complexity	simple	compound

The advantage of using this rating scale is not merely to assess the difficulty of a task, but to make it clear what you can do to make a specific task easier.

Let's look at some examples:

	cue	freq	per	win	pers	imp	com
appointments	1	1	1	1	0	0	0
special dates	1	1	1	1	0	0	0
returning books etc	1	0	0	0	0	0	0
shopping 1	0	0	0	0	0	0	0
shopping 2	0	1	0	1	1	1	1

Now, these ratings aren't carved in stone. An appointment may be unimportant to you, in which case it would score 5 instead of 4; it may be a frequent appointment, in which case it might score 3. Similarly, you may get out books or videos rarely, in which case the frequency would be rated 1, giving you a score of 2; you may not care if you don't return them on time, giving you an importance rating of 1 instead of 0.

Also, although I have, for the sake of consistency and simplicity, classified period of time simply as long-term or short-term, clearly there is a huge difference between, say, five minutes and three days, or one week and one year. Thus, a video or DVD that you have to return the next day may be easier to remember to return than one which you can have out for eight days.

Shopping, of course, is a very broad classification, which is why

I have given two extremes. The first rating is for buying your usual groceries for yourself and your family; the second is for buying an unimportant one-off item for yourself, for which you will need to do some research to find out exactly what you should get and where you should get it from.

So what does this exercise tell us? It tells us that appointments are hard to remember because they are time-based and have a narrow time-frame, and that they will be harder to remember when they are long-term, infrequent, and of relatively low importance to you. That special dates (which are usually annual), are hard to remember because they are time-based, have a narrow time-frame, are long-term and infrequent. In other words, the only thing they really have going for them is that they are (may be) important to you or to people you love.

It tells us that returning books/videos/DVDs is an easier time-based task than most, because it usually has a broad window, is short-term, important (you'll probably owe money if you forget), and habitual. The main factors determining ease are the extent to which the task is habitual, and the length of time you have to fulfill the task.

It tells us that shopping activities can vary widely in difficulty, depending chiefly on their frequency of occurrence and their complexity, as well as their degree of importance, whether they involve other people, and the length of time you have to complete the task.

Now let me reiterate: this is not a precise rating scale. Its function is to provide guidelines to help you *flexibly* judge your specific memory tasks, and points to those particular attributes you might wish to modify (if possible) or to concentrate on, in order to facilitate your remembering of that intention.

At the end of the book I have provided a blank table for you to fill in your own specific tasks.

Deciding on your memory strategies

On the next pages I give two examples of a personal worksheet for detailing your strategies for remembering intentions. The first looks at perennial memory tasks — the sort that come up again and again. But of course many tasks are one-offs, or at least very irregular in their occurrence. The second example looks at those.

To practice dealing with these situations, it's a good idea to start by writing down specific tasks facing you at the moment, and the very specific ways you think of for dealing with them. Keep writing them down as they occur until you are well-practiced and confident that you can use these strategies without prompting.

After you've studied these examples, check back to the quiz at the beginning of the book (if you printed out the downloadable sheet from my website this will be easier). Hopefully you now understand the meaning of each of those terms signified by the letters A-G, and you can point to any particular problem areas you have.

Memory task	Strategy
Remembering nieces' birthdays	Write their birth dates on birthday calendar
Remembering to return library books	Decide on a place in the house for library books and get into the habit of always putting them there
Remembering to pay bills on time	Decide on a regular day to do it on — make sure it's easy to remember. Mark it on the calendar for the first few months until habit established.
Remembering I need items that have run out	Get into the habit of putting empty containers on kitchen windowsill to remind me. Establish a shopping list on fridge door and get into habit of writing down items when I think of them.
Remembering phone calls I need to make	Decide on a suitable time for making phone calls — one for those which need to be made during business hours; one for personal. On the basis of where I'll be at that time, establish a place for putting reminder notes.
Remembering to take items when I go out	Make a place near the front door where items can be placed
Remembering what I need to do while out	Develop habit of running through items before leaving house. Count number of items and remember number.

Irregular memory task	Strategy
Remember to return Kilbirnie library books	Have partner drop books off when takes children to Kilbirnie pool. *Weekend — swimming pool — books*
Remember to write P a letter	Write myself a note. Stick it to computer.
Remember to ring the bank	Write a note. Stick it to PC.
Remember to put wart stuff on T's knee	Find an appropriate point in daily routine: when I'm reading to him before bed. *Storytime — warts*
Take car to garage in the morning	Take car key off key-ring and leave in my place at breakfast table.

It may be that your biggest problems aren't anything to do with prospective memory — they may be problems of short-term memory or attention, or of retrospective memory. Perhaps your biggest problems are confined to prospective memory tasks that involve other people (the problem there may be psychological rather than cognitive!), or perhaps they are organizational and/or motivational.

For those that are truly problems of intention (prospective) memory, write down the particular tasks you want to improve in the worksheet at the end of the book, and then, using the information provided in this book, write down your strategies for dealing with them. You may find it useful to look at the table in Appendix D (also available as a printable pdf sheet from my website at http://www.memory-key.com/books/planning-remember/resources), where I have briefly described strategies for dealing with most of the memory tasks mentioned in the quiz.

In the next, and last chapter, I'll look briefly at goal-setting problems — those I have dubbed "organization and/or motivational".

It's not all about memory

I want to end with a few words about non-memory issues that affect whether or not you carry out an intention. Because, while forgetting is assuredly the most common problem for achieving our intentions, it is not the sole problem.

For example, a study found that 70% of women who intended to carry out a breast self-examination but failed to do so, said they forgot[90] — making it clearly the most common problem, but leaving nearly a third who failed to carry out the intention for some other reason.

Let's look, very briefly, at those other problems.

We fail to achieve intentions for many reasons

Freud is responsible no doubt for the notion that we tend to forget intentions that we really don't want to do — an idea that presumably underlies the hurt you inflict when you forget to do something for someone you love.

However, a study that attempted to test this theory against the opposing one (that you'll in fact better remember intended actions that cause you strong discomfort, but fail to do them) found that, indeed, actions that were highly aversive were more likely to be remembered but not carried out$_{91}$.

> There's no evidence that forgetting to do something means we didn't want to do it.

And sometimes — a lot of the time! — we simply find it hard to force ourselves to do what we know we should do. We know we should go out for some exercise, but the day is dreary and we really don't feel like it. We know we should get out of bed, but it's so cozy, and once we get up, there's so much to do. We know we should start studying now and not leave it to the last minute, but we'd rather talk to friends/read a book/watch TV.

What we do might be driven by our intentions, but our intentions are not all on the same page! Some of our intentions are inconsistent; some are in competition. We want to be healthier, smarter, wealthier, happier, have more friends, have more time, have more fun ... These are broad goals most of us share, although each person will give these different priority values depending on their circumstances and personality.

> Achieving our goals isn't helped by the fact that they are not always consistent with each other.

It's hard to reconcile all of these, and it's especially hard to reconcile short- and long-term goals — what we want right now versus what we want eventually. As Saint Augustine famously wrote: "Give me chastity and continency, but not yet!"

But this isn't simply a matter of 'will power'. There are cognitive reasons why we sabotage ourselves.

The good and bad of habits

I have discussed how automatizing actions frees up your attentional capacity, and also how such automatization comes at a price (as seen in action slips). Habitual behavior affects not only such routine actions as those we discussed earlier, but also has implications for long-term intentions.

Goals are not only formed and pursued consciously — evidence suggests we can also have unconscious goals. In particular, it seems that, because goals act like any other concept in memory, the repeated linking of a goal with a particular situation will mean that when the situation occurs, the goal is automatically activated.

This is very useful, of course, as long as the goal is still held by the individual. In such a way, if you decide to always take the stairs instead of the elevator, the elevator will soon come to cue you automatically. This is, indeed, desirable, if you wish to establish this habit. However, if you find your knees can't take such activity and you should reduce how often you take the stairs, you are likely to keep finding yourself on the stairs anyway — as long as you are 'on automatic'.

> Actions designed to help us achieve a goal may become habitual. This can hinder our achieving a different goal, if the two are in opposition.

Goal commitment

But goals also differ in an important way from other mental concepts — they include a powerful motivational component. Most concepts, when activated, will fade with time. Goals, however, tend to grow *stronger* with time — because they seek resolution. It's this need for resolution that creates the tension we often feel when a goal is not achieved[92].

How determined a person is to achieve a particular goal is called goal commitment. Goal commitment is thought to be determined not only by the perceived value of the goal, but also by the person's expectation that they can actually achieve it. It's also assumed that a person will choose the method of achieving the goal that offers the best chance of success.

Actually, I'm not at all sure about this assumption — it's rather too reminiscent of the assumption economists made for so long, that people's behavior is based on rational choices (no wonder economic models were so unsuccessful!). But certainly the expectancy of achievement must play some part in selecting a means of achieving a goal.

Choice of means is also affected by how many means there are. Obviously, the more different ways there are of achieving a goal, the less chance any particular one has of being chosen.

So whether we achieve a goal depends on:

- how important it is to us
- how likely we believe we are to achieve it
- how effective the means we have chosen is
- how many different ways there are of achieving it
- how good our implementation plan is.

All these factors interact. For example, implementation plans are more likely to be effective if you have a strong commitment to achieving the goal, and to the plan itself. A study that varied the strength of participants' commitment to the plan by randomly telling some (after

> Whether we achieve a goal depends on how committed we are to it; this isn't simply a matter of how important it is to us.

giving them a personality test) that they were the type who would benefit from rigidly adhering to a plan, and telling others that they were the type who responded better to a more flexible approach, found that the latter (who presumably had a lower commitment to the plan) were less inclined to engage in the desired behavior when prompted by the situational cue$_{93}$.

Maintaining goal commitment

A major problem for long-term goals is of course the problem of maintaining them. All very well to start off committed and focused, but as the days turn into weeks and the weeks into months, it gets a lot harder to maintain that commitment.

Probably the most critical factor in determining your perseverance is whether you can see any progress towards your goal. This points to the importance of setting realistic progress goals — staging posts on your journey. It also suggests that feedback will be helpful.

Feedback, however, can be a two-edged sword. While objective feedback (feedback that tells you accurately how you're doing against your goals) is certainly helpful, it is not always motivating. Comparisons of older and younger adults, in particular, have shown that older adults do not always show improved goal performance when given objective feedback.

A lot of the problem can be seen as stemming from setting your goals at too high a level. In such cases, progress can be dispiriting, and you abandon your task. But this is not the fault of the progress! It is the goal level that's to blame.

Imagine, for example, the case of a sixty-year-old who wants to learn a new language. Being keen to see tangible results quickly, she decides her aim is to be able to get the gist of newspaper and magazine articles within three months. To achieve that, she decides she'll need to learn the top thousand words (in English, the first thousand words are said to cover 84% of conversation, 82% of fiction, and 76% of newspapers, so this seems a good aim). Dividing the number of words by the number of days, she calculates she needs to learn 11 new words a day, which seems easily achievable.

But it turns out that it is not as easy as all that. She starts off well, but after a while she realizes she's forgotten the ones she learned earlier. She realizes she needs to keep reviewing the old ones as well as learn new ones. Suddenly the task of learning 11 new words becomes learning 11 words and reviewing 110, 220, 330 ... And she tries to read something and realizes that even words she knows aren't always recognizable — she realizes she needs to know a lot of grammar, too. The job is becoming a lot harder, and here it is halfway through the second month and she's only learned 200 words!

And she thinks: "Maybe everyone is right; I'm too old to learn another language."

On the other hand, if her goals had been more realistic, she might have patted herself on the back, and said, "Everyone said I was too old to learn a new language, but look, I've already learned 200 words. I might beat my target of knowing the top 1000 words by the end of the year!"

Research suggests that people who don't have a strong belief in themselves and their abilities (and this includes many older people) will be more vulnerable to feedback that isn't positive. On the other hand, people with a strong belief in themselves are more likely to respond to negative feedback with increased motivation to try harder.

So you need to use this information to tailor your own goal

program. You should always strive to form realistic goals, but if you tend to be motivated by failure, you can afford to set more challenging goals. If, on the other hand, you easily lose your motivation when you don't do as well as you expected or hoped, then be generous in setting your progress goals. Make sure they are well within your grasp. If you think setting 'easy' goals is cheating somehow, assure yourself your ultimate goal is the same; all you are doing is setting smaller steps on the journey — and thus making it more likely that you will arrive at journey's end.

> Maintaining commitment to a goal requires you to see a level of progress that's acceptable to you.

What's important is that you can see that you're making progress.

But keeping yourself focused on your goal isn't just a commitment problem. There's also the problem of not being distracted by all the other things you want to do.

Distraction is perhaps a misleading word. Studies suggest it is not so much that people are distracted, as that people vary in their ability to cognitively inhibit alternative goals. One study, for example, found that the degree to which students were able to ignore the attractiveness of other activities was correlated with how well they were doing at college (measured by grade point average)[94].

Goals are often primed by the environment — a library might turn your mind to academic or literary goals (your intention to read *War and Peace*; your intention of learning a new language); a shopping mall to consumer goals (your intention to buy new shoes); the kitchen to food-related goals (your intention to prepare dinner). However, the goal primed by the environment may not be the one that was at the forefront of your mind. How often have you found yourself digressing from your original aim to something suggested by the environment you find yourself in?

Research suggests that when alternative goals are related to your main goal, they may in fact benefit your main goal by attracting more of your attentional and motivational resources. However, if the alternative goals are *un*related to your focal goal, they will pull resources away from that goal, making it less likely to be achieved.

> Your ability to stay focused on a goal depends on how easily distracted you are by alternative activities.

In such a way, your goal of *improving relations with the neighbor* might be helped by your goal of *tidying the garden* — but not by your goal of *spending more time at work*.

Individual differences

There are also personality factors that affect your ability to carry out your intentions.

People who are "state-oriented" are poor at regulating their emotions, especially in regard to generating positive emotion, and tend to hesitate and postpone difficult actions in difficult circumstances. Action-oriented people, on the other hand, tend to take actions in such circumstances relatively quickly. Accordingly, it is not surprising that these types of personality differ in their success at carrying out self-initiated tasks — that is, ones without external triggers.

> If you are a procrastinator, self-initiated tasks will be particularly difficult for you.

Studies[95] have found that, while state-oriented people are actually more likely to keep intentions in mind than those who are action-oriented, they are less likely to carry them out, especially when they have a number of intentions or are under time pressure. It's hypothesized that this is related to their difficulties in raising positive emotion, which may be needed to initiate the action. It's also suggested that the chronically repeated activation of an intention, without fulfilling it, actually inhibits its performance.

> A positive mood helps procrastinators achieve self-initiated intentions.

Research indicates then, that positive emotion is important for state-oriented people to carry out their intentions (but not for action-oriented people[96].

Procrastinators, therefore, should try to reduce the number of times they think of intended actions without doing anything about them, and make an effort to provide optimal conditions for carrying out the task: reduced time pressure (don't leave it till the last minute!); reduced number of tasks competing for attention (the longer you leave things, the more they'll pile up!); a good mood.

> Procrastination makes it harder to accomplish intentions.

As you can see, procrastination makes everything worse — the longer you put off doing something, the more times you will activate the intention without action; the more time pressure will increase; the more other intended tasks will accumulate. Three results, each one of which makes it harder to accomplish the task.

Believing in your abilities

What people believe about memory, and their own memory in particular, affects their memory abilities. This belief in your own memory abilities is affected in turn by:

- how well you believe your memory performs in various everyday situations

- how much you think your memory has changed in the past ten years
- how anxious memory situations make you
- how much you believe memory performance is under a person's control.

Memory for intentions is probably particularly important in forming (or undermining) your general faith in your memory — partly because failures can have such noticeable consequences, and partly because failures are often very apparent to other people.

How closely your memory beliefs match the reality of your memory depends in part on the familiarity of the task. In general, studies haven't found a good match between memory beliefs and actual performance, but there is some evidence that people are more reliable judges when the memory task is very familiar to them[97], and also quite specific. For example, your belief that you are poor at remembering people's names when you meet several people at once, is more likely to be true than the more general belief that you are poor at remembering people's names.

In such a way, you might think you're terrible at remembering to do things, not realizing (because your failures loom much larger in your memory than your successes) that you are in fact generally very good at remembering event-based tasks and broad-window time-based tasks, but that narrow-window time-based tasks are always difficult for you, and all prospective tasks are difficult when your routine is dramatically disrupted (such as when you go on vacation).

Interestingly, event- and time-based tasks may be influenced by different aspects of your beliefs. A study that compared the two found that the more you believe your memory is under your own control, the better you perform on event-based tasks. However, for time-based tasks, it was more important to believe in your memory abilities and their stability over the past ten years, and be less anxious in memory situations.

Whether you remember your intentions depends on the strategies you employ, and whether you make this effort depends in part on whether you believe this.

Time-based tasks are of course more demanding than event-based tasks. It is perhaps not surprising that people who have less faith in their abilities might feel overwhelmed by the more demanding task. And perhaps the connection between control beliefs and event-based tasks comes about because people who believe their memory is under their control are more likely to put deliberate effort into encoding the information needed[98].

The bottom line

So it comes back, as it always does, to strategies. I hope that, if nothing else, you come away from this book knowing that your ability to remember is in your hands. Some people may 'naturally' remember more easily; some people may notice some things are harder to remember as they get older. But none of this is a reason for you to fail to remember.

The only reason is that you can't be bothered to try.

I don't say that in an accusing way! There are many things I don't bother to remember. There is no inherent virtue in remembering everything. What's important is that you decide what's important to you to remember, and then choose the right strategies to help you do so.

And stop worrying about forgetting things you've decided aren't important!

Improving your memory is about training yourself in new habits. Effective habits. Specific habits, for specific situations.

You need to train yourself in specific strategies. You need to practice in specific situations. You need to train yourself to use appropriate strategies as a matter of habit.

Remembering is a skill.

A skill you can learn.

Appendix A: Theories of prospective memory

Is prospective memory fundamentally different from retrospective memory?

The very name for this future memory, the memory for intended actions, contrasts it with the "normal" memory of past occurrences: prospective memory, compared to retrospective memory. But to what extent is prospective memory different from retrospective memory?

One of the most obvious differences is that retrospective memory is normally triggered by something at the time of retrieval. Thus, you see a face, and are prompted to retrieve the associated name. You're asked a question, which prompts you to retrieve the answer. But in prospective memory, you are frequently obliged to remember something in the absence of an obvious prompt. Which leads to the burning question: how do we remember when there is nothing to prompt us?

Prospective memory may operate in a similar way to recognition

One approach to prospective memory suggests that it does in

fact operate in the same way as retrospective memory — that is, one aspect of retrospective memory, namely, recognition memory. Recognition memory is thought to be mediated by familiarity. Familiarity is, of course, a vital factor in memory processes, and it is assumed to be a function of:

- the number of times the stimulus has been experienced, and
- the length of time since it was last experienced.

Something that is already familiar will increase its familiarity only a very little when re-experienced; something that is not so familiar will be affected much more, when re-experienced. Thus, if you were shown a list of words, and then shown another list and asked to say which ones you had seen before, it would be harder to be certain about a word like *book* or *play* (because they are already so familiar, seeing them in the earlier list would have hardly increased their familiarity), while a word like *carousel* or *respiration* would be much easier to judge.

Familiarity judgments appear to occur automatically.

Prospective memory may work in a similar manner to recognition memory. That is, the familiarity of a target event (e.g., seeing a stationery shop) may prompt a memory search to determine its significance. If familiarity is high, a deeper memory search will begin, to determine the reason for the familiarity. The reason may then be revealed to be that the stimulus is a prospective memory target event. It may be, however, that the person decides it is familiar for some other reason. If familiarity isn't high enough, then, again, it will not be identified as a target event.

If prospective memory does indeed act in the same way as recognition memory, then other characteristics of recognition memory should also apply to prospective memory. For example, prospective memory should be better when the target event has been less frequently experienced (the impact of re-experiencing it will be greater) — and this is true$_{99}$.

Some aspects of prospective memory do NOT resemble the recognition process

However, it does not appear that prospective memory operates exactly like recognition memory. Increasing the familiarity of a target event by repeatedly presenting it appears to have no effect on prospective memory$_{100}$. That is, repeating to yourself "remember the news", for example, doesn't help you remember whatever action you intend to do when you hear / watch the news.

A modification to this theory suggests that it is not the familiarity of the target events *per se* that is important in prospective memory. What is important is the link between target event and intended action. And indeed, repeated reminders that link target event to intended action (e.g., "remember to turn on the oven after the news") do have a positive effect on prospective memory$_{101}$.

Theory explains many characteristics of prospective memory

This theory further assumes that prospective memory is supported by a memory process termed the automatic associative memory module (thought to reside in the hippocampus). According to this theory, when you notice a target event, it is processed in this module. If the target event interacts with the intended action, then out pops the idea that you need to do whatever. If it doesn't interact (because the link between the target event and the intended action is not strong enough), then you fail to remember what you meant to do.

This accounts for a number of characteristics of prospective memory that research has uncovered:

- why older adults are as good as younger adults at remembering simple event-based prospective memory tasks (because the process is automatic)
- why reminders of only the target event fail to improve prospective memory (because it is the interaction between event and action that is important)
- why successful prospective remembering is typically immediate upon presentation of the target event (the length of time it takes to retrieve information from memory is usually a significant variable in memory research)
- typical reports from subjects that they engaged in no particular strategy, the memory just "popped into mind"
- the lack of effect of dividing attention at retrieval on event-based prospective memory (in most memory tasks, being required to attend to more than one task does make retrieval slower or more difficult; however, it shouldn't affect an automatic process).

Not all characteristics of prospective memory are accounted for by the theory

However, there are some findings that are not immediately

explained by this theory. For example, the lack of effect of dividing attention at retrieval referred to above applies only to younger adults. Older adults *are* affected by having to do another task while retrieving an intended action.

It is suggested that this reflects the role of the frontal lobes in prospective memory, specifically, that part of it involved in working memory. Working memory is needed to hold an intended action in memory once it has been retrieved, working out how to perform the various tasks required, and monitoring that performance. Thus, it is thought that it is not the initial retrieval of the intended action that is affected by the distraction, but the keeping it in mind while trying to perform other tasks. If so, having to hold on to the thought of the intention for a short period should be much harder for older adults than younger, and so, indeed, it appears. This applies even to very short delays (10 seconds).

The frontal area of the brain appears to be particularly vulnerable to aging.

The demands of other activities impacts on the ease of keeping an intention in mind

According to this view, then, anything that places additional demands on working memory (dividing attention, maintaining an intended action in memory over a short delay, simultaneously performing a task that is particularly demanding for older adults) should disadvantage older adults to a greater extent than younger adults. It also follows that even younger adults will be hindered in remembering intentions if the demands on working memory are sufficiently great. Both these consequences are supported by research$_{102}$. (To be more specific, event-based prospective memory can be disrupted in younger adults if they are simultaneously required to do something that uses central executive working memory resources, e.g., planning and monitoring, but not when the task uses non-executive working memory resources, such as repeating words aloud).

It must be remembered that prospective memory usually operates in a situation where we are distracted by other activities. The trick of remembering intentions is to remember them in the hurly-burly of daily life.

Theory accounts for intentions cued by events, but what about when we try to remember?

While this theory appears quite successful in explaining event-based prospective memory, it does not completely account for how prospective memory works. Not all intended actions are triggered automatically — sometimes we go in search for them. When we search memory for actions we planned to do, the situation is more akin to a free recall task than a recognition task.

Where the situation differs from a typical retrospective memory task is that prospective memory tasks occur against a background of another activity. The person remembering has two competing tasks, and some sort of resolution process must take place to decide which task will be carried out. Thus, the more committed you are to the ongoing activity which must be interrupted to carry out the prospective memory task, the less likely you are to perform the prospective memory task.

Moreover, an intended action differs from other actions in that it must have the "flavor" of an intention, a *goal*. The representation of the action in memory — the memory code — must be tagged "goal". There are various possible ways in which this might occur. For example, goals might be kept active in a "goal stack", either in working memory or a specific "scheduling component" in the frontal lobes.

Another possibility is that target actions are retrieved from permanent memory, in the same way as any memory, and every action is automatically checked against a goal list.

It may also be that both possibilities are correct, for different situations.

How does remembering time-based intentions fit into this?

Whatever the length of time for which you must remember the intention, as the due date gets closer, your behavior changes. Thus, a month before the event, the precise hour of an appointment will be of less interest to you than the due day. The hour becomes more important as the event approaches. Similarly, when you put a cake in the oven, you will check the time increasingly often as the time approaches its expected finish$_{103}$.

A mechanism by which we perform such time-monitoring in the short-term has been theorized to involve a Test-Wait-Test-Exit (TWTE) loop: you test whether the time has come for the action; if it hasn't, you set a Wait period that is to elapse before you test it again. If the Wait period turns out to be too short, you can reset it.

Conclusion

It seems likely that prospective memory shares elements with retrospective memory, but that there are important differences. In particular, that:

- a prospective memory task is a task that is secondary to another task,
- a remembered action must have the status of a goal,
- performance of the prospective memory task requires the target action to be strong enough to interrupt the main task, and
- scheduling is one of the most important aspects for prospective memory.

Appendix B: External memory aids

As the demands on our memory grow, so too does the market for high-tech memory aids to help us deal with it all. Computers provide various facilities for reminders, such as calendar systems, to-do task lists, temporal document lists (systems that organize documents temporally can provide reminders about what you are working on, and can be used proactively to remind you to work on something; sophisticated systems can even allow you to add documents in a future part of the document stream).

Increasingly, cellphones and palmtops also provide reminder facilities. Watches can now be found that provide multiple alarm settings. Pillboxes are available that signal reminders, as well as being organized in such a way as to tell you if you have already taken the appropriate medication. The TimePAD is a pocket size timer that enables you to record up to 5 short reminder messages and set the alarm to play your message at the right time. The iPhone has a number of apps to help you remember intended tasks and planned events (e.g., Things, Todo, Remember the milk, Goal tender, reQall).

Such reminders, however, are all based on time triggers. This is, of course, much easier from the point of technology, and it also deals directly with the main problem we have with remembering intentions — time-based intentions are much harder to remember than tasks that are cued by some event.

However, many of our intentions in daily life are triggered by place rather than time.

Context-based reminder systems

New reminder systems are getting much smarter. The new breed, still in development, is trying to deal with the far more complex task of being able to remind you of your intention not simply at the right time, but when you are in the right place or circumstance.

Thus, the MemoClip, a device that can be clipped to your shirt, containing a computer, some sensors, communication capabilities and a LCD display (4x5 cm). The MemoClip communicates with "LocationBeacons", solar panel powered, connectionless devices installed in your environment so that it knows where you are at any given time, and matches your location against a stored list of tasks. When you're near a location associated with a task, the device beeps, and the text of the appropriate reminder is called up on the small display screen. The tasks are entered in a PC program, which also has encoded descriptions of known places, plus possible relationships between places. Information is easily downloaded from the PC program to the MemoClip.

Usability studies of the MemoClip have found the biggest potential problems are: (1) the way notification information is entered into the system, and (2) the way location is described. Location descriptions appear to be subject to constant change. The inventor is working on ways to accommodate this, and also to answer users' desire for location to be linked with time.

Another device, the CybreMinder, allows you to specify

conditions under which to remember a task, like taking an umbrella to work if (a) it is cloudy and (b) someone else needs the car. This system doesn't involve a wearable device, but does require more devices to be installed in the environment. The system receives information from temperature and location sensors, cameras and speech recognition units. When it senses the appropriate conditions for a task, it reminds you using e-mail, a pop-up window on the nearest device display, or synthesized speech on the cellphone.

Yet another system in the early stages of development is the Memory Glasses, another wearable system. The glasses are wired with a display that enables reminder messages to be seen, and are worn in conjunction with a jacket fitted with computing, sensing and speech recognition equipment. This device is also intended to have other memory capabilities, such as recognizing people.

These devices are aimed most particularly at those who have memory damage of various kinds. I cannot imagine those with normal memory needing or wanting such intrusive and effortful aids. However, development of such technologies may well teach us more about the ways in which people encode and recall intentions.

References

Beigl, M. 2000. MemoClip: A Location based Remembrance Appliance. 2th International Symposium on Handheld and Ubiquitous Computing (HUC 2000), Bristol, UK, Sept. 25-27, 2000 and Personal Technologies, 4 (4), Springer Press, pp. 230-234F. http://www.teco.edu/~michael/publication/memoclip/ http://www.teco.edu/~zimmer/memoclip.php

DeVaul, R.W., Pentland, A. & Corey, V.R. 2003. The Memory

Glasses: Subliminal *vs.* Overt Memory Support with Imperfect Information. 7th IEEE International Symposium on Wearable Computers October 21-23, 2003. http://www.media.mit.edu/wearables/mithril/memory-glasses.html

Dey, A.K. & Abowd, G.D. 2000.Minder: A Context-Aware System for Supporting Reminders. In P. Thomas and H.-W. Gellersen (eds.) International Symposium on Handheld and Ubiquitous Computing (HUC 2000), pp. 172-186. www.cc.gatech.edu/fce/contexttoolkit/pubs/HUC2000.pdf

Appendix C: The coding mnemonic

Coding mnemonics are used for encoding numbers. Because words are much easier for most of us to remember, a system that transforms numbers into letters is one of the best ways for remembering numbers.

Here is one such coding system:

1 = t (there is 1 downstroke in t)

2 = n (there are 2 downstrokes in n)

3 = m (there are 3 downstrokes in m)

4 = r (r is the last letter of four)

5 = l (l is 50 in Roman numbers)

6 = sh (six has a sort of sh sound)

7 = k (number 7 is embedded in k)

8 = f (both 8 and f have two loops)

9 = p (9 is p the wrong way round)

0 = s (zero starts with a s sound)

The codes are not arbitrary. They have been chosen with a view to facilitating rote memorization. As you can see however, some of the rationales are somewhat contrived. You are not obliged to memorize a coding system that is given to you. There is no particular superiority in any one set of digit-letter equivalences over another. But if you are modifying a coding system by substituting equivalences you find more obvious, you need to bear in mind confusability. For example, an equivalence between *f* and *5* might seem obvious, but there is a strong likelihood of becoming confused between *4* and *5* when decoding.

Once encoded into letters, the numbers can then be incorporated into words or rhymes. Only consonants are used for coding. Vowels are then inserted as necessary. Thus the 5th of January could be coded as *lout* or *let* or *loot*; the 23rd of December could be *name ten*. If your sister Mary's birthday is on January 5, you could remember it with the mnemonic *Let Mary* or *Mary is a lout*. Your marriage to Jim on December 23 could be remembered as *Name ten bad days I've had with Jim*.

You can read more about the coding mnemonic and its applications in my book *Mnemonics for Study*.

Appendix D: Specific strategies for specific tasks

Memory task	Strategy
Remembering comments or questions during conversation	practice finding a quick label or keyword for the idea, and repeat this label/word several times at intervals
Remembering all the items you need when at the supermarket	write down items as I think of them; practice the habit of remembering to take it; practice the habit of checking it before going to the checkout
Remembering all your errands	plan the order in which the errands should be done, mentally visualizing the trip, emphasizing the places where I have to stop. Back-stop with a list.
Remembering to take medication at the right time	before starting the medication, sort out the best time to take it (in accordance with any medical instructions), making sure it ties in with a landmark event
Remembering casual, short-term intentions	always rehearse the intention
Remembering appointments	note on the calendar; practice the habit of regularly checking the calendar

Remembering special dates	keep a birthday calendar; remember to mark down all dates to remember; remember to turn it at the end of every month
Remembering promises you make to other people	always write them down, or if appropriate, use an environmental aid to trigger recall
Remembering to return library books / DVDs on time	put books / DVDs that are ready to return in a specific place near the door
Remembering routine chores	always do them at the same time (preferably after a landmark event); if prevented, use an environmental aid to trigger later recall
Remembering infrequent personal tasks	decide when it will be done and make a note on the calendar
Remembering personal goals	decide on specific, progressive goals and set a regular time to do it
Remembering work goals	decide on specific actions and note them in the appropriate check-list; practice the habit of regular review (set a regular time)
Remembering ideas	think up a label/keyword that will cue recall, and link it to a relevant memory
Remembering to pass on information to others	make a note immediately; if not possible, rehearse until you can

Glossary of terms

action slips: forgetting actions that you do routinely. Absent-mindedness (failure of attention) rather than true forgetting.

associative memory module: according to a model by Moscovitch (1994), explicit episodic memories involve several subsystems, one of which — a module in the hippocampal area — is involved in the encoding, storage, and retrieval of associations. The searching of associations by this module is assumed to occur automatically.

complexity: a way of defining intention tasks in terms of what other activities are being simultaneously engaged in

domains: systems within memory that process different kinds of information. For example, facts, faces, events, emotions, skills, and intentions, are all different kinds of information that need to be dealt with in different ways.

encoding: the process of transforming information into a memory code, and placing it in your long-term memory

environmental aids: any object that helps you to remember, such as Post-it notes, shopping lists, calendars, diaries, alarms, knots in your handkerchiefs, objects placed prominently, etc.

event-based task: in which a cue (for example, seeing a shop, or a person, or a book) prompts you to remember your intention

frontal lobes: the frontal lobes (left and right) are situated at the "front" of the cortex, i.e. behind the forehead. They are the largest of the four lobes in the cerebrum, and may be thought of as the "highest" part of our brain. The frontal lobes are critical for those faculties that humans regard as special to our species - reasoning, planning, some aspects of language.

hippocampus: means "sea horse", and is named for its shape. It is one of the oldest parts of the brain, and is buried deep inside, within the temporal lobe. It is part of the limbic system. The hippocampus is important for the forming, and perhaps long-term storage, of associative and episodic memories. Specifically, the hippocampus has been implicated in (among other things) the encoding of face-name associations, the retrieval of face-name associations, the encoding of events, the recall of personal memories in response to smells.

implementation plans: if-then plans that connect what would be good opportunities to fulfill an intention with the action required to achieve that intention. They differ from simple intentions in that they specify the context in which the intentions can occur.

landmarks: events that are significant in your life, that help you date events in your past.

monitoring: strategies to inform you how well you have learned the information in a memory situation so that you can plan your encoding strategies appropriately

plan generation: thinking about novel ways of achieving your goals

predictive encoding: a strategy to enhance your recall of intended actions by encoding your intentions in terms of later opportunities.

prospective memory: memory for intentions, for actions we wish or expect to carry out in the future; contrasts with retrospective memory.

pulse: an intended action that must be performed at a specific time, or within a very narrow time frame

recall: the retrieval of information from long-term memory

recognition: the awareness that you have seen or learned this information before

retrieval cues: things that prompt you to recall certain memories.

retrieving: finding a memory code; "remembering"

retrospective memory: memory of information from the past (most memory falls into this category); contrasts with prospective memory.

sequencing errors: an error in a well-practiced action sequence, such as repeating or omitting an element, or carrying it out in the wrong place in the sequence.

situational awareness: learning what to notice in a target situation

step: an intended action that can be performed at any time within a broad time frame

target situation: the circumstances in which an intended activity is to be carried out

time-based task: in which you have to remember your intention, without any prompts, after a specific period has elapsed (for example, checking the oven after half an hour)

working memory: includes the part of memory of which you are conscious; the "active state" of memory. Information being "put into" memory is held in working memory; memories being remembered are held in working memory. The capacity of working memory — how much information it can hold at one time — is severely limited. Working memory governs your ability to comprehend what you are reading or hearing, your ability to learn new words, your ability to plan and organize yourself, and much more.

working memory capacity: the amount of information you can hold and work with at one time

Chapter Notes

[1] Crovitz & Daniel 1984; Terry 1988.

[2] Intons-Peterson & Newsome 1992

[3] Self-reports on various questionnaires have shown little correlation with actual performance on memory tasks in most studies (Herrmann, 1982). People's perceptions of how their memory has changed over time has also shown little correlation with actual changes in performance. It has been speculated that memory questionnaires may indicate the *trust* people have in their memory, rather than their memory performance. Similarly, it has been speculated that perceptions of memory change with age reflect the person's beliefs about how memory changes with age, rather than any actual change.

Memory beliefs also seem to be influenced by social relationships. One study found that husbands' self-reports of their memory performance agreed completely with the reports from their wives (Hertzog & Dunlosky 1996). However, there was little agreement between the husbands' reports of their wives' memory performance and the women's self-reports. Does this indicate a lack of knowledge or a lack of influence? Perhaps a little of both!

[4] Hertzog et al. 2000.

[5] In general, studies have reported little correlation between performance on prospective and retrospective tasks (e.g., Einstein & McDaniel, 1990; Kvavilashvili, 1987; Maylor 1990;

Wilkins & Baddeley, 1978). Indeed, one study found that those who performed poorly at a task where they were required to recall a list of words (a retrospective task) performed better on a prospective memory task than those who performed well on the recall task! (Wilkins & Baddeley 1978). It is common to find little correlation in the performance of different memory tasks (see e.g., Morris 1984), and this is considered to support the view that there is not a general memory ability.

For that matter, performance on different types of retrospective memory task also varies. For example, a study of performance on 31 laboratory memory tasks found separate factors for free recall, paired-associate learning, memory span, and verbal discrimination (Underwood et al. 1978); a questionnaire study of everyday memory abilities found at least eight different memory factors (Herrmann & Neisser, 1978). Today, researchers tend to talk about different memory skills, rather than someone having a "good" memory.

[6] Morris 1992.

[7] Kvavilashvili 1987

[8] Foerde, Knowlton & Poldrack 2006

[9] Gazzaley et al. 2005

[10] Colcombe et al. 2005

[11] Colcombe et al. 2003; Colcombe et al. 2004

[12] Colcombe & Kramer 2003

[13] Erickson et al. 2007

[14] Witelson, Kigar & Stoner-Beresh 2001

[15] Eldridge, Sellen & Bekerian 1992

[16] Reason 1990, p70

[17] Norman 1981

[18] William James (1890): the classic text, *Principles of Psychology*

[19] Botvinick, M.M. & Bylsma, L.M. 2005

[20] Robertson et al. 1997

[21] Hashstroudi, Johnson & Chrosniak 1990; Cohen & Faulkner 1989

[22] Broadbent, D.E., Cooper, P.F., Fitzgerald, P. & Parkes, K.R. 1982

[23] Yamasaki, LaBar & McCarthy 2002

[24] Broadbent et al. 1982

[25] Brett, M. & Baxendale, S. 2001 Poser (1986) Parsons & Redman (1991)

[26] Casey 2000; Janes et al 1999

[27] Casey, P. 2000. Janes et al (1999) Brindle et al (1991)

[28] Drummond et al. 1999

[29] Drummond, Gillin & Brown 2001

[30] Larson, G.E. & Perry

[31] Boomsma, D.I. 1998

[32] Smith-Spark et al

[33] Rabbitt, P.M.A. & Vyas, S.M. 1980. Rabbitt, P.M.A. 1981.

[34] Dosher & Lu 2005

[35] Carter et al. 2005

[36] Lavie 2005

[37] Sheeran and Orbell (2000)

[38] Searleman & Herrmann 1994

[39] Einstein et al. 2000

[40] Brandimonte & Passolunghi 1994

[41] Ellis & Milne 1996

[42] Okuda et al. 2000

[43] Brandimonte & Passolunghi 1994

[44] Marsh & Hicks 1998

[45] Kvavilashvili 1987

[46] Walbaum 1997

[47] Einstein, Smith, McDaniel & Shaw 1997

[48] Kvavilashvili 1987

[49] Meacham & Singer 1977

[50] Meacham & Kushner 1980

[51] Altgassen et al 2009

[52] Meacham & Leiman 1982

[53] Ellis 1988

[54] Maylor 1990.

[55] Watanabe, Okabe & Kawaguchi 1999; Watanabe & Kawaguchi 1999; Leirer, Decker Tanke. & Morrow 1994; Wilkins & Baddeley 1978.

[56] Watanabe & Kawaguchi 1999

[57] Ellis 1988; Ellis & Nimmo-Smith 1993

[58] Brandimonte & Passalonghi 1994 reported that intervening activities during a short delay led to interference; Kvavilashvili 1987 found that such activities interfered only with unimportant intentions; Ellis & Nimmo-Smith 1993 found that the activity engaged in during the interval was a factor for remembering intentions over long intervals.

[59] Harris 1984

[60] Moscovitch 1982; Harris & Sunderland 1981; Poon & Shaffer 1982

[61] Jackson et al. 1988

[62] Einstein & McDaniel 1991

[63] Einstein & McDaniel 1996

[64] Kliegel, McDaniel & Einstein 2000

[65] Driscoll, McDaniel & Guynn 2005

[66] Singer et al. 2006

[67] Schack, Klimesch & Sauseng 2005

[68] Goschke & Kuhl 1993; 1996

[69] Searleman 1996

[70] Ellis and Ashbrook's (1988) *Resource Allocation Model*

[71] Eysenck and Calvo's (1992) *Processing Efficiency Theory*

[72] Heffernan et al. 2005; Heffernan et al. 2001; Heffernan, Moss & Ling 2002

[73] Bisiacchi 2000; Ouriache 2000; Brooks et al. 2002; Kopp & Thöne. 2000; Quayle 2000; Groot et al. 2002; Hannon et al. 1995; Roche, Fleming & Shum 2002; Kerns 2000

[74] Martin et al. 2000

[75] Harris, Cumming & Menzies 2000; Shum, Toivanen & Hohaus 2000

[76] Smith & Bayen 2005; Smith & Bayen 2004

[77] Intons-Peterson & Fournier 1986

[78] In one study, some participants were told that they would be reminded to do the required tasks, while others were asked to

remind another participant, and others weren't told anything about reminding. Those who were led to expect a reminder remembered significantly fewer of the tasks they were asked to do. To a lesser extent, those who had been asked to remind others remembered more tasks that those who were not (Schaefer & Laing 2000)

[79] Schwartz, Wand, Zeitz & Goss 1962

[80] Park & Mayhorn 1996

[81] Doherty et al. 1983

[82] Patalano & Seifert 1997

[83] Guynn, McDaniel & Einstein 1998

[84] Guynn, McDaniel & Einstein 1998

[85] Intons-Peterson & Fourrier 1986

[86] Gates & Colborn 1976

[87] Levy & Claravall 1977

[88] Liu & Park 2004

[89] Wilkins & Baddeley 1978

[90] Orbell, Hodgkins & Sheeran 1997

[91] Meacham & Kushner 1980

[92] Carver & Scheier, 1998; Miller, Galanter, & Pribram, 1960; Goschke & Kuhl, 1993; Liberman, Förster, & Higgins, 2005; Bargh et al. 2001

[93] Sheeran, Webb & Gollwitzer 2005

[94] Locke & Kristof 1996

[95] Goschke & Kuhl 1996; Beswick &Mann 1994; Blunt & Pychyl 1998; Stiensmeier-Pelster 1994

[96] Kazén, Kaschel & Kuhl 2008

[97] West, Berry, & Powlishta (1986)

[98] McDonald-Miszczak 1999

[99] Einstein & McDaniel 1990.

[100] Guynn, McDaniel & Einstein 2001.

[101] Guynn, McDaniel & Einstein 2001.

[102] Maylor, 1993; 1996 found older adults perform more poorly than younger adults on a simple event-based prospective memory task, if they are simultaneously required to remember famous names (retrieving names is a particularly demanding task for older adults). McDaniel, Robinson-Riegler & Einstein 1998, and Marsh & Hicks 1998, have both found that even younger adults are hindered by having to divide their attention (by simultaneously performing another task) while remembering an event-based prospective memory task.

[103] Ceci & Bronfenbrenner 1985 found, in fact, that children waiting for cupcakes to cook, made several time checks in the first five minutes, few in the middle fifteen minutes, and many in the last five minutes. Similar results were found by Harris & Wilkins 1982, who had their adult subjects watch a two hour video, during which they were to hold up a card from a pile of cards at the time specified on the card. It was speculated that the initial time-checks were to calibrate their internal clock. Further experiments in which clocks designed either to decelerate or accelerate were used, found that, when the clocks were too far from the subjects' expectations, time-checks were constant through the period (Ceci, Baker & Bronfenbrenner 1988).

References

Altgassen, M., Kliegel, M., Brandimonte, M. & Filippello, P. 2009. Are older adults more social than younger adults? Social importance increases older adults' prospective memory performance. *Aging, Neuropsychology, and Cognition, 17, 312-28..*

Bargh, J.A., Gollwitzer, P.M., Lee-Chai, A., Barndollar, K. & Trötschel, R. 2001. The automated will: Nonconscious activation and pursuit of behavioral goals. *Journal of Personality and Social Psychology, 81,* 1014-27.

Beswick, G., &Mann, L. 1994. State orientation and procrastination. In J. Kuhl & J. Beckmann (Eds.), *Volition and personality: Action versus state orientation* (pp. 391–396). Göttingen: Hogrefe.

Bisiacchi, P.S. 2000. Prospective memory in Parkinson's disease. In L. Kvavilashvili & J. Ellis (Ed.), 1st International Prospective Memory Conference, Hatfield, Hertfordshire, U.K. University of Hertfordshire Press.

Blunt, A., & Pychyl, T. A. 1998. Volitional action and inaction in the lives of undergraduate students: State orientation, boredom, and procrastination. *Personality and Individual Differences, 24* (6), 837-846.

Boomsma, D.I. 1998. 1998. Genetic analysis of cognitive failures (CFQ): a study of Dutch adolescent twins and their parents. *European Journal of Personality, 12* (5), 321-330.

Botvinick, M.M. & Bylsma, L.M. 2005. Distraction and action slips in an everyday task: Evidence for a dynamic representation of task context. *Psychonomic Bulletin & Review, 12 (6)*, 1011-17.

Brandimonte, M.A.& Passolunghi, M.A. 1994. The effect of cue-familiarity, cue-distinctiveness, and retention interval on prospective remembering. *Quarterly Journal of Experimental Psychology, 47A*, 565-587.

Brett, M. & Baxendale, S. 2001. Motherhood and Memory: A Review. *Psychoneuroendocrinology, 26*, 339-362.

Brindle, P.M., Brown, M.W., Brown, J., Griffith, H.B. and Turner, G.M. 1991. Objective and subjective memory impairment in pregnancy. *Psychological Medicine, 21*, 647-653.

Broadbent, D.E., Cooper, P.F., Fitzgerald, P. & Parkes, K.R. 1982. The Cognitive Failures Questionnaire (CFQ) and its correlates. *British Journal of Clinical Psychology, 21*, 1-16.

Brooks, B.M., Rose, F.D., Potter, J., Attree, E.A., Jayawardena, S. & Morling, A. 2002. Assessing stroke patients' ability to remember to perform actions in the future using virtual reality. Proceedings of the 4th International Conference on Disability, Virtual Reality & Associated Technology, Veszprém, Hungary.

Carter, O.L., Presti, D.E., Callistemon, C., Ungerer, Y., Liu, G.B., and Pettigrew, J.D. 2005. Meditation alters perceptual rivalry in Tibetan Buddhist monks. *Current Biology, 15*, R412-R413.

Carver, C.S. & Scheier, M.F. 1998. *On the self-regulation of behaviour*. Cambridge, UK: University Press.

Casey, P. 2000. A longitudinal study of cognitive performance during pregnancy and new motherhood. *Archives of Women's Mental Health, 3 (2)*, 65-76.

Ceci, S.J., Baker, J.G. & Bronfenbrenner, U. 1988. Prospective remembering and temporal calibration. In In M.M. Gruneberg, P.E. Morris, & R.N. Sykes (eds). *Practical Aspects of Memory: Current Research and issues. Vol. 1.* Chichester: Wiley.

Ceci, S.J. & Bronfenbrenner, U. 1985. "Don't forget to take the cupcakes out of the oven": Prospective memory strategic time-monitoring and context. *Child Development, 56,* 152-64.

Cohen, G. & Faulkner, D. 1989. Age differences in source forgetting: Effects on reality monitoring and on eyewitness testimony. *Psychology and Aging, 4,* 10-17.

Colcombe, S.J., Erickson, K.I., Raz, N., Webb, A.G., Cohen, N.J., McAuley, E. & Kramer, A.F. 2003. Aerobic Fitness Reduces Brain Tissue Loss in Aging Humans. *Journal of Gerontology: Series A: Biological and Medical Sciences, 58,* M176-M180.

Colcombe, S.J., Kramer, A.F., Erickson, K.I. & Scalf, P. 2005. The Implications of Cortical Recruitment and Brain Morphology for Individual Differences in Inhibitory Function in Aging Humans. *Psychology and Aging, 20(3),* 363-375.

Colcombe, S.J., Kramer, A.F., Erickson, K.I., Scalf, P., McAuley, E., Cohen, N.J., Webb, A., Jerome, G.J., Marquez, D.X. & Elavsky, S. 2004. Cardiovascular fitness, cortical plasticity, and aging. *PNAS, 101,* 3316-3321.

Crovitz, H. F., & Daniel, W. F. 1984. Measurements of everyday memory: Toward the prevention of forgetting. *Bulletin of the Psychonomic Society, 22,* 413-414.

Dodhia, R.M. & Dismukes, R.K. 2009. Interruptions create prospective memory tasks. *Applied Cognitive Psychology, 23 (1),* 73-89.

Doherty, W.J., Schrott, H.B., Metcalf, L. & Iasiello-Vailas, L. 1983. The effects of spouse support and health beliefs on medication adherence. *Journal of Family Practice, 17,* 837-41.

Dosher, B.A. & Lu, Z-L. 2005. Perceptual learning in clear displays optimizes perceptual expertise: Learning the limiting process. *PNAS, 102,* 5286-5290.

Driscoll, I., McDaniel, M.A. & Guynn, M.J. 2005. Apolipoprotein E and Prospective Memory in Normally Aging Adults. *Neuropsychology, 19 (1)*, 28-34.

Drummond, S.P.A., Brown, G.G., Stricker, J.L., Buxton, R.B., Wong, E.C. & Gillin, J.C. 1999. Sleep deprivation-induced reduction in cortical functional response to serial subtraction. *NeuroReport, 10 (18)*, 3745-3748.

Drummond, S.P.A., Gillin, J.C. & Brown, G.G. 2001. Increased cerebral response during a divided attention task following sleep deprivation. *Journal of Sleep Research, 10 (2)*, 85-92.

Einstein, G.O. & McDaniel, M.A. 1990. Normal aging and prospective memory. *Journal of Experimental Psychology: Learning, Memory, and Cognition, 16*, 717-26.

Einstein, G.O. & McDaniel, M.A. 1991. Aging and time- versus event-based prospective memory. Paper to the 32nd annual meeting of the Psychonomic Society, San Francisco. Reported in Morris 1992.

Einstein, G.O. & McDaniel, M.A. 1996. Remembering to do things: Remembering a forgotten topic. In D. Herrmann, M. Johnson, C. McEvoy, C. Hertzog & P. Hertel (eds.) *Research on Practical Aspects of Memory Vol. 2*, 79-93. NJ: Lawrence Erlbaum Associates.

Einstein, G. O., McDaniel, M. A., Manzi, M., Cochran, B., & Baker, M. 2000. Prospective memory and aging: Forgetting intentions over short delays. *Psychology and Aging, 15(4)*, 671–683.

Einstein, G.O., Smith, R.E., McDaniel, M.A. & Shaw, P. 1997. Aging and prospective memory: The influence of increased task demands at encoding and retrieval. *Psychology and Aging, 12*, 479-88.

Eldridge, M., Sellen, A. & Bekerian, D. 1992. Memory Problems at Work: Their Range, Frequency and Severity. Rank Xerox Research Centre: Technical Report EPC-1992-129. http://research.microsoft.com/~asellen/publications/memory%20problems%2092.pdf

Ellis, J.A. 1988. Memory for future intentions: Investigating pulses and steps. In M.M. Gruneberg, P.E. Morris, & R.N. Sykes (eds). *Practical Aspects of Memory: Current Research and issues. Vol. 1. Memory in everyday life.* Chichester: Wiley. pp 371-6.

Ellis, J., & Milne, A. 1996. Retrieval cue specificity and the realization of delayed intentions. *Quarterly Journal of Experimental Psychology (A): Human Experimental Psychology, 49(4)*, 862–887.

Ellis, J.A. & Nimmo-Smith, I. 1993. Recollecting naturally-occurring intentions: A study of cognitive and affective factors. *Memory, 1*, 107-26.

Erickson, K.I., Colcombe, S.J., Elavsky, S., McAuley, E., Korol, D., Scalf, P.E. & Kramer, A.F. 2007. Interactive effects of fitness and hormone treatment on brain health in postmenopausal women. *Neurobiology of Aging, 28 (2)*, 179-185.

Foerde, K., Knowlton, B.J. & Poldrack, R.A. 2006. Modulation of competing memory systems by distraction. *Proceedings of the National Academy of Sciences, 103*, 11778-11783.

Förster, J., Liberman, N., & Higgins, E.T. 2005. Accessibility from active and fulfilled goals. *Journal of Experimental Social Psychology, 41*, 220-239.

Gates, S.J. & Colborn, D.K. 1976. Lowering appointment failures in a neighbourhood health center. *Medical Care, 14*, 263-7.

Gazzaley, A., Cooney, J.W., Rissman, J. & D'Esposito, M. 2005. Top-down suppression deficit underlies working memory impairment in normal aging. *Nature Neuroscience, 8*, 1298-1300.

Goschke, T. & Kuhl, J. 1993. Representation of intentions: Persisting activation in memory. *Journal of Experimental Psychology: Learning, Memory, & Cognition, 19,* 1211-26.

Goschke, T. & Kuhl, J. 1996. Remembering what to do: Explicit and implicit memory for intentions. In M.A. Brandimonte, G.O. Einstein & M.A. McDaniel (eds). *Prospective memory: Theory and applications* (pp 1-22). Hillsdale, NJ: Erlbaum.

Groot, Y.C.T., Wilson, B.A., Evans, J. & Watson, P. 2002. Prospective Memory Functioning In People With And Without Brain Injury. *Journal of the International Neuropsychological Society, 8 (5),* 645-654.

Gruneberg, M.M. 1992. The practical applications of memory aids: knowing how, knowing when, and knowing when not. In M.M. Gruneberg, & P. Morris (eds). *Aspects of memory. Vol.1: The practical aspects.* 2nded. London: Routledge.

Gruneberg, M. M. & Herrmann, D. J. 1997. *Your memory for life!* London: Blandford.

Guynn, M.J., McDaniel, M.A. & Einstein, G.O. 2001. Remembering to perform actions: A different type of memory? In H.D. Zimmer, R.L. Cohen, J. Engelkamp, R. Kormi-Nouri, & M.A. Foley (eds.) *Memory for action: A distinct form of episodic memory?* Oxford University Press. pp.25-48.

Guynn, M.J., McDaniel, M.A. & Einstein, G.O. 1998. Prospective memory: When reminders fail. *Memory & Cognition, 26,* 287-298.

Hannon, R., Adams, P., Harrington, S., Fries-Dias, C. and Gibson, M. T. 1995. Effects of brain injury and age on prospective memory self-rating and performance. *Rehabilitation Psychology, 40,* 289–297.

Harris, J.E. 1984. Remembering to do things: A forgotten topic.

In J.E. Harris & P.E. Morris (eds.) *Everyday memory, Actions and Absentmindedness*. London: Academic Press.

Harris, L.M., Cumming, S.R. & Menzies, R.G. 2000. Resource allocation and prospective memory test performance. In L. Kvavilashvili & J. Ellis (Ed.), 1st International Prospective Memory Conference, Hatfield, Hertfordshire, U.K. University of Hertfordshire Press.

Harris, J.E. & Sunderland, A. 1981. Effects of age and instructions on an everyday memory questionnaire. Paper presented to the British Psychological Society Cognitive Psychology Section Conference on Memory, Plymouth.

Harris, J.E. & Wilkins, A.J. 1982. Remembering to do things: A theoretical framework and illustrative experiment. *Human Learning, 1*, 123-36.

Hashstroudi, S., Johnson, M.K. & Chrosniak, L.D. 1990. Aging and qualitative characteristics of memories for perceived and imagined complex events. *Psychology and Aging, 5*, 119-126.

Heffernan, T.M., Ling, J., Parrott, A.C., Buchanan, T., Scholey, A.B. & Rodgers, J. 2005. Self-rated everyday and prospective memory abilities of cigarette smokers and non-smokers : a web-based study. *Drug and alcohol dependence, 78 (3)*, 235-241.

Heffernan, T.M, Jarvis, H., Rodgers, J., Scholey, A.B. & Ling' J. 2001. Prospective memory, everyday cognitive failure and central executive function in recreational users of Ecstasy. *Human Psychopharmacology, 16(8)*, 607-61.

Heffernan, T.M., Moss, M. & Ling, J. 2002. Subjective ratings of prospective memory deficits in chronic heavy alcohol users. *Alcohol and Alcoholism, 37 (3)*, 269-271.

Herrmann, D.J. 1982. Know thy memory: The use of questionnaires to assess and study memory. *Psychological Bulletin, 92*, 434-52.

Herrmann, D.J. & Neisser, U. 1978. An inventory of everyday memory experiences. In M.M. Gruneberg, P.E. Morris & R.N. Sykes (eds). *Practical Aspects of Memory*. NY: Academic Press.

Hertzog, C. & Dunlosky, J. 1996. The aging of practical memory: An overview. In D.J. Herrmann, C. McEvoy, C. Hertzog, P. Hertel, & M.K. Johnson (eds.) *Basic and Applied Memory Research, Vol.2: Theory in Context*. Mahwah, NJ: Lawrence Erlbaum Associates.

Hertzog, C., Park, D.C., Morrell, R.W. & Martin, M. 2000. Ask and ye shall receive: behavioural specificity in the accuracy of subjective memory complaints. *Applied Cognitive Psychology, 14*, 257-275.

Intons-Peterson, M.J. & Fournier, J. 1986. Environmental and internal memory aids: when and how often do we use them? *Journal of Experimental Psychology: General, 115*, 267-280.

Intons-Peterson, M.J. & Newsome, G.L. III. 1992. Environmental memory aids: effects and effectiveness. In D. Herrmann, H. Weingartner, A. Searleman & C. McEvoy (eds.) *Memory Improvement: Implications for Memory Theory*. New York: Springer-Verlag.

Jackson, J.L., Bogers, H. & Kerstholt, J. 1988. Do memory aids aid the elderly in their day to day remembering? In M.M. Gruneberg, P.E. Morris & R.N. Sykes (eds) *Practical aspects of memory: Current research and issues, v.1*. Chichester: Wiley.

James, W. 1890. Principles of Psychology. Available at http://psychclassics.yorku.ca/James/Principles/index.htm

Janes, C., Casey, P., Huntsdale, C. & Angus, G. 1999. Memory in pregnancy. I: Subjective experiences and objective assessment of implicit, explicit and working memory in primigravid and primiparous women. *Journal of psychosomatic obstetrics and gynaecology, 20(2)*, 80-87.

Kazén, M., Kaschel, R. & Kuhl, J. 2008. Individual differences in intention initiation under demanding conditions: Interactive effects of state vs. action orientation and enactment difficulty. *Journal of Research in Personality, 42 (3)*, 693–715.

Kerns, K.A. 2000. A comparison of prospective memory in children with and without ADHD using the CyberCruiser paradigm. In L. Kvavilashvili & J. Ellis (Ed.), 1st International Prospective Memory Conference, Hatfield, Hertfordshire, U.K. University of Hertfordshire Press.

Kliegel, M., McDaniel, M.A., & Einstein, G.O. 2000. Plan formation, retention, and execution in prospective memory: A new approach and age-related effects. *Memory & Cognition, 28*, 1041-9.

Kopp, U.A. & Thöne, A.I.T. 2000. Role of executive functions and memory processes in delayed intentions after head injury. In L. Kvavilashvili & J. Ellis (Ed.), 1st International Prospective Memory Conference, Hatfield, Hertfordshire, U.K. University of Hertfordshire Press.

Kvavilashvili, L. 1987. Remembering intention as a distinct form of memory. *British Journal of Psychology, 78*, 507-18.

Larson, G.E. & Perry, Z.A. 1999. Visual capture and human error. *Applied Cognitive Psychology, 13 (3)*, 227-236.

Lavie, N. 2005. Distracted and confused?: Selective attention under load. *Trends in Cognitive Sciences, 9(2)*, 75-82.

Leirer, V.O., Decker Tanke, E. & Morrow, D.G. 1994. Time of day and naturalistic prospective memory. *Experimental Aging Research, 20 (2)*, 127-134.

Levy, R.L. & Claravall, V. 1977. Differential effects of a phone reminder on patients with long and short between-visit intervals. *Medical Care, 15*, 435-8.

Liu, L.L. & Park, D.C. 2004. Aging and Medical Adherence: The Use of Automatic Processes to Achieve Effortful Things. *Psychology and Aging, 19 (2)*, 318–325.

Locke, E.A. & Kristof, A.L. 1996. Volitional choices in the goal achievement process. In P.M. Gollwitzer & J.A. Bargh (eds.), *The psychology of action: Linking cognition and motivation to behaviour.* (pp. 365-384). New York: Guilford Press.

Marsh, R.L. & Hicks, J.L. 1998. Event-based prospective memory and executive control of working memory. *Journal of Experimental Psychology: Learning, Memory, and Cognition, 24,* 336-49.

Martin, M., Kliegel, M., McDaniel, M.A. & Einstein, G.O. 2000. The neuropsychology of prospective memory: The role of central executive functions. In L. Kvavilashvili & J. Ellis (Ed.), 1st International Prospective Memory Conference, Hatfield, Hertfordshire, U.K. University of Hertfordshire Press.

Maylor, E.A. 1990. Age and prospective memory. *The Quarterly Journal of Experimental Psychology, 42A,* 471-93.

Maylor, E.A. 1993. Aging and forgetting in prospective and retrospective memory tasks. *Psychology and Aging, 8,* 420-8.

Maylor, E.A. 1996. Age-related impairment in an event-based prospective-memory task. *Psychology and Aging, 11,* 74-8.

McDaniel, M.A., Robinson-Riegler, B. & Einstein, G.O. 1998. Prospective remembering: Perceptually-driven or conceptually-driven processes? *Memory & Cognition, 26,* 121-34.

McDonald-Miszczak, L. 1999. Metamemory predictors of prospective and retrospective memory performance. *Journal of General Psychology, 126 (1),* 37-52.

McEvoy, C.L. 1992. Memory improvement in context: Implications for the development of memory improvement theory. In D. Herrmann, H. Weingartner, A. Searleman & C. McEvoy (eds.) *Memory Improvement: Implications for Memory Theory*. New York: Springer-Verlag.

Meacham, J.A. & Kushner, S. 1980. Anxiety, prospective remembering, and performance of planned actions. *Journal of General Psychology, 103*, 203-9.

Meacham, J.A. & Leiman, B. 1982. Remembering to perform future actions. In U. Neisser (ed.) *Memory observed: Remembering in natural contexts*. pp 327-36. San Francisco: Freeman.

Meacham, J.A. & Singer, J. 1977. Incentive effects in prospective remembering. *Journal of Psychology, 97*, 191-7.

Miller, G.A., Galanter, E. & Pribram, K.A. 1960. *Plans and the structure of behavior*. New York: Holt, Rhinehart, & Winston.

Morris, P.E. 1984. The validity of subjective reports of memory. In J.E. Harris & P.E. Morris (eds.) *Everyday memory, Actions and Absentmindedness*. London: Academic Press

Morris, P.E. 1992. Prospective memory: remembering to do things. In M.M. Gruneberg, & P. Morris (eds.) *Aspects of memory. Vol. 1: The practical aspects*. 2nd ed. London: Routledge.

Moscovitch, M. 1982. A neuropsychological approach to memory and perception in normal and pathological aging. In F.I.M. Craik & S. Trehub (eds). *Aging and cognitive processes*. NY: Plenum.

Norman, D. A. 1981. Categorization of action slips. *Psychological Review. 88(1)*, 1-14.

Okuda, J., Fujii, T., Yamadori, A., Ohtake, H., Tsukiura, T., Suzuki, K., Kawashima, R., Fukuda, H. & Itoh, M. 2000. Brain regions responsible for time-based and event-based prospective memory tasks: a positron emission tomography study. In L.

Kvavilashvili & J. Ellis (Ed.), 1st International Prospective Memory Conference, Hatfield, Hertfordshire, U.K. University of Hertfordshire Press.

Orbell, S., Hodgkins, S. & Sheeran, P. 1997. Implementation intentions and the theory of planned behavior. *Personality and Social Psychology Bulletin, 23,* 945-954.

Ouriache, S.J. 2000. Executive dysfunction in schizophrenia: An explanation of deficits in prospective memory? In L. Kvavilashvili & J. Ellis (Ed.), 1st International Prospective Memory Conference, Hatfield, Hertfordshire, U.K. University of Hertfordshire Press.

Park, D.C. & Mayhorn, C.B. 1996. Remembering to take medications: the importance of nonmemory variables. In D. Herrmann, M. Johnson, C. McEvoy, C. Hertzog & P. Hertel (eds.) *Research on Practical Aspects of Memory Vol. 2,* 95-110, NJ: Lawrence Erlbaum Associates.

Parsons, C. and Redman, S. 1991 Self-reported cognitive change during pregnancy. *Australian Journal of Advanced Nursing, 9,* 20-29.

Patalano, A.L. & Seifert, C.M. 1997. Opportunistic planning: Being reminded of pending goals. *Cognitive Psychology, 34,* 1-36.

Poon, L.W. & Shaffer, G. 1982. Prospective memory in young and elderly adults. Paper presented to the American Psychological Association, Washington D.C.

Poser, C.M., Kassirer, M.R. and Peyser, J.M. (1986) Benign encephalopathy of pregnancy. Preliminary clinical observations. *Acta Neurologica Scandinavica, 73,* 39-43.

Quayle, A.H. 2000. Prospective memory in the real world: Which abilities are the best predictors in a head-injured sample? In L. Kvavilashvili & J. Ellis (Ed.), 1st International Prospective

Memory Conference, Hatfield, Hertfordshire, U.K. University of Hertfordshire Press.

Rabbitt, P.M.A. 1981. Cognitive psychology needs models for changes in performance with old age. In A. Baddeley & J. Long (Eds.), *Attention and performance IX*. Hillsdale, N.J.: L. Erlbaum Associates.

Rabbitt, P.M.A. & Vyas, S.M. 1980. Selective anticipation for events in old age. *Journal of Gerontology*, 35, 913-919.

Reason, J.T. 1984. Absent-mindedness and cognitive control. In J.E. Harris & P.E. Morris (eds.) *Everyday memory, Actions and Absentmindedness*. London: Academic Press

Reason, J.T. 1990. *Human Error*. New York: Cambridge University Press.

Robertson, I. H., Manly, T., Andrade, J., Baddeley, B.T., & Yiend, J. 1997. 'Oops!': Performance correlates of everyday attentional failures in traumatic brain injured and normal subjects. *Neuropsychologia*, 35, 747-758.

Roche, N.L., Fleming, J.M. & Shum, D.H.K. 2002. Self-awareness of prospective memory failure in adults with traumatic brain injury. *Brain Injury*, 16 (11), 931-945.

Schack, B., Klimesch, W. & Sauseng, P. 2005. Phase synchronization between theta and upper alpha oscillations in a working memory task. *International Journal of Psychophysiology*, 57(2), 105-114.

Schaefer, E.G. & Laing, M.L. 2000. 'Please, remind me …': The role of others in prospective remembering. *Applied Cognitive Psychology*, 14 (7), S99-S114. (Special Issue: New Perspectives in Prospective Memory. Issue Edited by Lia Kvavilashvili, Judi Ellis.)

Schwartz, D., Wand, M., Zeitz, L. & Goss, M.E. 1962.

Medication errors made by elderly chronically ill patients. *American Journal of Public Health, 52,* 2018-29.

Searleman, A. 1996. Personality variables and prospective memory performance. In D. Herrmann, M. Johnson, C. McEvoy, C. Hertzog & P. Hertel (eds.) *Research on Practical Aspects of Memory Vol. 2,* 95-110, NJ: Lawrence Erlbaum Associates.

Searleman, A. & Herrmann, D. 1994. *Memory from a broader perspective.* NY: McGraw-Hill.

Sheeran, P. & Orbell, S. 2000. Using implementation intentions to increase attendance for cervical cancer screening. *Health Psychology, 19,* 283-9.

Sheeran, P., Webb, T.L. & Gollwitzer, P.M. 2005. The Interplay Between Goal Intentions and Implementation Intentions. *Personality and Social Psychology Bulletin, 31 (1),* 87-98.

Shum, D., Toivanen, A. & Hohaus, L. 2000. Effect of working-memory demand on prospective memory in young, young-old, and old-old individuals. In L. Kvavilashvili & J. Ellis (Ed.), 1st International Prospective Memory Conference, Hatfield, Hertfordshire, U.K. University of Hertfordshire Press.

Singer, J.J, Falchi, M., MacGregor, A.J., Cherkas, L.F. & Spector, T.D. 2006. Genome-wide scan for prospective memory suggests linkage to chromosome 12q22. *Behavior Genetics, 36 (1),* 18-28.

Smith, R.E. & Bayen, U.J. 2004. A Multinomial Model of Event-Based Prospective Memory. *Journal of Experimental Psychology: Learning, Memory, and Cognition, 30 (4),* 756–777.

Smith, R.E. & Bayen, U.J. 2005. The Effects of Working Memory Resource Availability on Prospective Memory: A Formal Modeling Approach. *Experimental Psychology, 52(4),* 243-256.

Smith-Spark, J.H., Fawcett, A.J., Nicolson, R.I. & Fisk, J.E. 2004.

Dyslexic students have more everyday cognitive lapses. *Memory*, 12 (2), 174-82.

Stiensmeier-Pelster, J. 1994. Choice of decision-making strategies and action versus state orientation. In J. Kuhl & J. Beckmann (Eds.), *Volition and personality* (pp. 167–176). Göttingen, Germany: Hogrefe & Huber.

Terry, W. S. 1988. Everyday forgetting: Data from a diary study. *Psychological Reports, 62,* 299-303.

Underwood, B.J., Boruch, R.F. & Malmi, R.A. 1978. Composition of episodic memory. *Journal of Experimental Psychology: General, 107 (4)*, 393-419.

Walbaum, S.D. 1997. Marking Time: The Effect of Timing on Appointment Keeping. *Applied Cognitive Psychology, 11 (4)*, 361-368.

Watanabe, H. & Kawaguchi, J. 1999. The effect of time of day on memory for plans. The Second International Conference on Cognitive Science.

Watanabe, H., Okabe, Y., & Kawaguchi, J. 1999. How do we remember our future plan?: Memory of schedule. *The third biennial meetings of the Society for Applied Research in Memory and Cognition.*

West, R. L., Berry, J. M., & Powlishta, K. K. 1986. Self-efficacy and performance on laboratory and everyday memory tasks. Paper presented at the meeting of the Gerontological Society of America, Chicago.

Wilkins, A.J. & Baddeley, A.D. 1978. Remembering to recall in everyday life: An approach to absent-mindedness. In M.M. Gruneberg, P.E. Morris, & R.N. Sykes (eds.) *Practical aspects of memory* (pp. 27-34). London: Academic Press.

Witelson, S.F., Kigar, D.L. & Stoner-Beresh, H.J. 2001. Sex

difference in the numerical density of neurons in the pyramidal layers of human prefrontal cortex: a stereologic study. Paper presented to the annual Society for Neuroscience meeting in San Diego, US.

Woll, S. 2002. Everyday thinking: Memory, reasoning, and judgment in the real world. NJ: Lawrence Erlbaum Associates.

Yamasaki, H., LaBar, K.S. & McCarthy, G. 2002. Dissociable prefrontal brain systems for attention and emotion. *Proceedings of the National Academy of Sciences USA, 99(17)*, 11447-51.

Zimmer, H.D. 2001. Why do actions speak louder than words? Action memory as a variant of encoding manipulations or the result of a specific memory system? in H.D. Zimmer, R.L. Cohen, J. Engelkamp, R. Kormi-Nouri, & M.A. Foley (eds.) *Memory for action: A distinct form of episodic memory?* Oxford University Press. pp151-98.

www.ingramcontent.com/pod-product-compliance
Lightning Source LLC
Chambersburg PA
CBHW071356290426
44108CB00014B/1570